Career Manifestation

Career Manifestation

Aligning Your Professional Path with Your Personal Purpose

Published in 2024

ISBN: 9789358810837 (PB)
ISBN: 9789358812473 (eBook)

Published by

Mindful Pages
Imprint of Alpha Editions LLC
312 W. 2nd St #1834
Casper, WY 82601, USA
www.mindfulpagespublishers.com

Contents

Introduction 1

Chapter 1: Understanding Manifestation and Career Alignment 4

Chapter 2: Discovering Your Personal Purpose 16

Chapter 3: Setting Intentional Career Goals 27

Chapter 4: Overcoming Obstacles and Mindset Shifts 43

Chapter 5: Practical Steps for Career Manifestation 57

Chapter 6: Navigating Career Transitions with Manifestation 69

Chapter 7: Maintaining Alignment and Purpose Over Time 82

Conclusion 96

About the Author 102

Introduction

In a world where the pursuit of a meaningful career has become more paramount than ever, this book serves as a beacon for those at the crossroads of their career journey. This insightful book delves deep into the essence of career manifestation—a process that transcends traditional job searches and career advancements, rooting itself in the profound alignment of one's professional path with their innermost values and purpose.

From the foundational understanding of manifestation and its application to career alignment in Chapter 1 to the concluding reflections on maintaining this alignment over time, this book offers a comprehensive guide through the transformative journey of crafting a career that is not only successful but deeply fulfilling. Each chapter, meticulously designed, builds upon the last, creating a step-by-step pathway for readers to follow.

Whether you find yourself questioning your current career trajectory, seeking to discover your true personal purpose, or navigating the complex waters of career transitions, this book offers valuable insights and practical strategies to guide you. Through the exploration of intentional goal setting, overcoming obstacles, and the continuous evolution of personal growth and professional aspirations, "Career Manifestation" invites you to embark on a journey of self-discovery and empowerment.

Embrace the journey within these pages, and allow it to guide you towards a career that resonates with your soul, aligns with your values, and brings to life the deepest expressions of your personal purpose. Welcome to the path of career manifestation.

In the pursuit of a career that resonates deeply with our personal values and purpose, the principle of manifestation emerges as a potent and transformative tool. Far from being mere wishful thinking, manifestation is the deliberate practice of bringing our desired reality into being through the power of focused intention, belief, and action. It invites us to not only envision the career alignment we seek but to actively participate in its creation, shaping our professional paths with intention and clarity.

The Power of Intention

At the core of manifestation lies the power of intention. Setting a clear, focused intention is the first step in aligning our careers with our values and purpose. This intentional thought acts as a beacon, guiding our actions and decisions towards the fulfillment of our professional aspirations. By defining what alignment looks like for us—whether it's working in a role that matches our skills and passions, contributing to a cause we care deeply about, or achieving a balance between our work and personal life—we set the stage for manifestation to unfold.

Belief: The Catalyst for Change

Belief is the fuel that powers the engine of manifestation. It's about harboring an unwavering conviction in the possibility of achieving alignment, even when faced with challenges or setbacks. This belief nurtures a mindset of possibility and openness, essential for recognizing and seizing the opportunities that lead us closer to our desired career path. By cultivating a deep-seated belief in our worth, capabilities, and the attainability of our goals, we energize our intentions and attract the circumstances conducive to their realization.

Aligned Action: Bridging Thought and Reality

Manifestation transcends mere thought; it necessitates action—action that is aligned with our intentions and beliefs. This involves taking concrete steps towards our career goals, whether by acquiring new skills, networking with industry professionals, or applying for roles that align with our values and purpose. Aligned action is purposeful and directed, a physical manifestation of our commitment to achieving career alignment. It closes the gap between where we are and where we aspire to be, turning the vision of our ideal career into a tangible reality.

The Role of Visualization and Affirmations

Visualization and affirmations are powerful techniques in the manifestation toolkit, helping to reinforce our intentions and beliefs. Through visualization, we create a vivid mental image of our aligned career, experiencing the emotions and success as if they were already ours. Affirmations, meanwhile, are positive statements that reaffirm our ability to manifest our goals, bolstering our belief and motivation. Together, these practices keep our focus sharp and our spirits high, ensuring that our energy remains aligned with our aspirations.

Embracing the Journey of Manifestation

Manifestation is as much about the journey as it is about the destination. It encourages us to embrace each step of our career path with mindfulness and gratitude, learning and growing from every experience. As we navigate the waters of professional development, manifestation serves as a compass, ensuring that we remain true to our values and purpose, even as they evolve over time.

In essence, manifestation is a powerful tool for achieving career alignment, offering a holistic approach that blends intention, belief, and action. By harnessing the principles of manifestation, we empower ourselves to create a career that not only meets our professional aspirations but also resonates with the deepest parts of who we are. Through manifestation, we can transform the vision of an aligned career from a distant dream into a lived reality, marking each step forward with purpose, passion, and fulfillment.

Chapter 1: Understanding Manifestation and Career Alignment

Manifestation, a term that has found resonance beyond its metaphysical origins, is increasingly being recognised for its profound implications in the spheres of career development and personal growth. At its core, manifestation is the process through which individuals can bring their deepest aspirations into tangible reality through the power of focused thought, intention, and action. It is a concept that harmonises the esoteric with the pragmatic, suggesting that our inner world—our thoughts, beliefs, and emotions—holds the key to transforming our external circumstances. This principle, when applied to career alignment, offers a revolutionary approach to achieving professional fulfilment and success.

The art of career manifestation is not about mere wishful thinking or the simplistic notion of attracting wealth and status. It is a nuanced process that requires an intimate understanding of one's personal values, strengths, and purposes. In this context, manifestation acts as a bridge between one's inner desires and their external professional world, enabling individuals to not only achieve their career goals but also ensure that these goals are in harmony with their deeper life purpose. This alignment is crucial, for a career that resonates with one's personal values and passions is more likely to yield satisfaction and a sense of accomplishment.

The psychological foundation of manifestation is rooted in the understanding that our thoughts have the power to shape our reality. This idea, while ancient in its origin, has found backing through various psychological theories and research. Cognitive psychology, for instance, provides insight into how our beliefs and expectations can influence our perceptions and actions. When we focus our thoughts and energies on specific career goals, we become more attuned to the opportunities that align with these objectives. This heightened awareness is critical in navigating the complex landscape of career development, allowing us to seize opportunities that we might otherwise overlook.

The theoretical underpinnings of manifestation also draw from the concept of the self-fulfilling prophecy, wherein one's expectations about an outcome can inadvertently cause that outcome to occur. In the realm of career development, this means that positive beliefs and expectations about one's professional journey can actually propel one towards achieving those expectations. This is not to suggest that success is merely a matter of positive thinking; rather, it is the alignment of belief, intention, and action that catalyses the manifestation process. The alignment of one's career with their personal purpose requires not only a clear vision of what one wants to achieve but also an unwavering belief in the possibility of its attainment.

Moreover, the practice of manifestation in career development is complemented by the concept of flow, a state in which individuals are fully immersed and engaged in their activities, experiencing a profound sense of joy and fulfilment. Achieving flow in one's career implies that the work one does is not only aligned with their skills and interests but also challenges them in a way that is neither too daunting nor too mundane. This state of flow is indicative of a career that is not only successful in conventional terms but also deeply fulfilling on a personal level.

The process of aligning one's career with their personal purpose through manifestation also involves a critical examination of one's environment. The spaces we inhabit, the people we surround ourselves with, and the daily practices we engage in can all influence our ability to manifest our desired career outcomes. A supportive environment, one that reflects and reinforces our career aspirations, can significantly enhance our manifestation efforts. This involves creating a physical space that inspires productivity and creativity, cultivating a professional network that is supportive and aligned with our goals, and adopting daily practices that keep us focused and motivated.

Furthermore, manifestation necessitates a dynamic approach to career development. In an ever-changing professional landscape, the ability to adapt and realign one's career aspirations with evolving personal values and market realities is paramount. This adaptability is not a departure from the manifestation process but rather an integral part of it. Manifestation, in this sense, is not a one-time act but a continuous process of growth, self-reflection, and realignment.

The practice of career manifestation offers a holistic approach to professional development, one that emphasises the importance of aligning one's career with their personal purpose. This alignment is not merely about achieving external markers of success but about finding joy, fulfilment, and meaning in one's work. By understanding and applying the principles of manifestation, individuals can navigate their career paths with intention, harnessing the power of their thoughts and actions to create a professional life that resonates with their deepest values and aspirations. In doing so, they not only contribute to their own personal growth but also to the broader societal good, embodying the true essence of success.

Unveiling the Power of Manifestation: Steering Your Career and Personal Growth to New Heights

In the contemporary lexicon of personal and professional development, 'manifestation' emerges as a concept both intriguing and profoundly impactful. It beckons the question: How can one harness the intangible—thoughts, intentions, and aspirations—to mould the tangible realities of their career and personal life? Manifestation, when dissected within the framework of career progression and personal growth, transcends the boundaries of mere ambition, evolving into a deliberate process of transforming one's professional desires into palpable outcomes through focused intention and concerted action.

The essence of manifestation lies in its simplicity and the profound belief that our inner world—our thoughts, aspirations, and beliefs— holds the key to influencing our external environment. In career and personal growth, this principle advocates for a harmonious alignment between one's professional objectives and their deepest personal values and growth ambitions. Such alignment is not serendipitous but a product of meticulous intention and action, a testament to the power of manifestation in creating a fulfilling professional journey.

To manifest a career that not only advances professionally but also resonates on a personal level requires an acute awareness of one's values, strengths, and, fundamentally, what one seeks to achieve in their life beyond the confines of job titles and financial gain. This understanding paves the way for setting career goals that are not only ambitious but also deeply intertwined with the fabric of one's personal identity and aspirations for growth. The act of aligning career aspirations with personal growth objectives is a deliberate manifestation strategy, ensuring that each step taken in one's professional journey contributes not only to external success but to internal development and satisfaction.

The process of manifestation in this dual arena involves several key stages, beginning with the clarity of intention. Knowing precisely what one desires in their career—whether it's a particular role, the impact one wishes to have in their field, or the values they want their work to embody—is the foundation upon which manifestation is built. This clarity of vision enables individuals to set intentions that are both specific and imbued with personal significance, thereby enhancing the motivational drive to achieve them.

Following intention, the role of visualization cannot be overstated. Visualization in the context of career manifestation involves creating a vivid mental image of the desired outcome, complete with the emotions and senses one associates with achieving that goal. This practice not only reinforces one's commitment to their career aspirations but also primes the mind to identify and seize opportunities that align with those goals. It is a powerful tool in bridging the gap between desire and reality, leveraging the subconscious mind's ability to influence decision-making and action towards the envisioned outcome.

Action, however, remains the critical conduit through which intentions and visualizations materialize into reality. Manifestation is not a passive process; it demands proactive steps towards the desired career trajectory. This involves not only the obvious actions such as networking, skill development, and seeking opportunities but also the more nuanced aspects of manifestation such as aligning one's daily habits, decisions, and even the company one keeps, with their career and personal growth goals.

Furthermore, manifestation in the sphere of career and personal development is a dynamic process. It requires an ongoing alignment of actions with evolving intentions and values. This dynamic nature of manifestation acknowledges that as individuals grow and evolve, so too do their career aspirations and definitions of personal success. The ability to adapt one's manifestation strategies in response to this evolution is crucial in maintaining the relevance and effectiveness of the manifestation process over time.

Moreover, the impact of aligning career goals with personal values and growth ambitions extends beyond the attainment of professional milestones. It fosters a deeper sense of fulfillment, purpose, and well-being. When one's career trajectory is a true reflection of their personal values and aspirations for growth, work becomes more than a means to an end; it transforms into a source of joy, inspiration, and personal development. This alignment ensures that the pursuit of professional success contributes to, rather than detracts from, one's overall quality of life and personal satisfaction.

The journey of career manifestation, guided by the principles of intention, visualization, and action, is a testament to the power of aligning one's professional path with their personal growth and values. It is a process that not only enhances professional fulfillment but also enriches one's personal development, highlighting the indelible link between who we are, who we aspire to be, and the career paths we choose to embark upon. Manifestation, in this light, is not just about achieving career success; it is about creating a life of purpose, fulfillment, and continuous growth.

Intuition: Your Compass in the Career Manifestation Journey

In the intricate dance of career progression, where the steps between success and stagnation can often seem choreographed by external forces, intuition emerges as a profound inner guide. This article embarks on an exploration of intuition's pivotal role in career decisions and the manifestation process, proposing a harmonious alliance between the cerebral act of rational decision-making and the often-underestimated power of our inner guidance system. Intuition, in its essence, offers a channel to opportunities that resonate more deeply with our personal purpose and values, acting as a compass in the vast ocean of career possibilities.

Intuition, or what many might refer to as a 'gut feeling', is a cognitive process more intricate than mere emotional reaction. It is the brain's way of drawing on past experiences, patterns, and external cues, often without our conscious awareness, to inform decisions that feel instinctively 'right'. In the context of career manifestation, where the alignment of one's professional path with their personal values is paramount, intuition can serve as a critical tool. It aids in sifting through the cacophony of societal expectations, peer pressure, and the myriad of options that the professional world presents, guiding us towards choices that truly resonate with our core.

The balance between rational decision-making and intuition is akin to a dialogue between the mind and the soul. Rational decision-making, with its emphasis on logical analysis, pros and cons, and tangible outcomes, is undeniably crucial in planning a career. It allows for structured planning, goal setting, and the mitigation of risks. However, this analytical approach, when operating in isolation, can sometimes lead us down paths that, while seemingly perfect on paper, lack resonance with our deeper aspirations. Herein lies the value of intuition. It provides the missing piece in the career decision-making puzzle, offering insights that, although difficult to quantify, are invaluable in their ability to guide us towards our true purpose and passion.

The manifestation of a fulfilling career is often a journey of aligning one's professional ambitions with personal values and purpose. Intuition plays a key role in this alignment, acting as a guide to identifying opportunities that not only promise success in traditional terms but also fulfilment and satisfaction on a personal level. When intuition and rationality work in concert, the decision-making process becomes more holistic, taking into account not only the external metrics of success but also the internal sense of purpose and joy that truly fulfilling careers provide.

The cultivation of intuition as a tool in career manifestation requires mindfulness and self-awareness. It involves creating spaces of silence and reflection in our often hectic lives, allowing the subtle voice of our inner guidance to emerge and be heard. This might entail practices such as meditation, journaling, or simply spending time in nature—activities that slow down the external noise and enable us to connect with our inner selves. The more attuned we become to our intuition, the more confidently we can navigate the complexities of career decisions, trusting in our inner compass to guide us towards choices that align with our deepest values and aspirations.

Moreover, intuition can lead us to explore and seize unconventional opportunities that rational analysis might overlook. It encourages a readiness to venture into the unknown, driven by a deep-seated belief in the alignment between our personal values and the opportunities we choose to pursue. This openness to intuition-led opportunities is where the magic of manifestation truly unfolds, allowing for career paths that are not only successful but also uniquely ours, imbued with personal significance and fulfilment.

The integration of intuition into the career manifestation process does not diminish the value of rational decision-making but rather complements it, offering a more rounded approach to career development. It recognises that while career paths can be planned, analysed, and strategised, there is also a space for the spontaneous, the unexpected, and the intuitively aligned opportunities that can lead to the most fulfilling professional experiences.

The role of intuition in career manifestation is akin to navigating by the stars. It requires faith in the unseen, a willingness to trust in our inner guidance, and the courage to follow where it leads. This journey, guided by both intuition and rationality, allows for the discovery of career paths that are not only successful in conventional terms but are also deeply resonant with our personal purpose and values. It is in this harmony between the mind and the soul that the true essence of career manifestation lies, offering a path to professional fulfilment that is both meaningful and rewarding.

In essence, intuition is not just a supplementary tool in our career decision-making toolkit; it is a fundamental aspect of navigating our professional journeys. It encourages us to look beyond the immediate and the tangible, urging us to consider what truly matters in the long run. By honouring our intuition as we manifest our career aspirations, we open ourselves up to a world of possibilities that align more closely with who we are and what we wish to achieve, both professionally and personally.

The Mind's Magnet: Unraveling the Science Behind Manifestation

The fascinating journey of manifestation, from an esoteric practice to a subject of psychological inquiry, offers a rich terrain for exploring the confluence of ancient wisdom and contemporary science. This article delves into the psychological and theoretical frameworks that underpin the effectiveness of manifestation, particularly in the domain of career advancement and personal growth. By weaving together cognitive psychology concepts and the principles of the law of attraction, we can begin to understand how the mind acts as a powerful magnet, attracting opportunities that resonate with our deepest aspirations and goals.

At the heart of manifestation lies the reticular activating system (RAS), a bundle of nerves at our brainstem that filters out unnecessary information, allowing us to focus on what is important. The RAS is instrumental in the manifestation process because it enables us to notice opportunities and resources that align with our goals. When we set a clear intention or goal, the RAS begins to highlight information, people, and opportunities related to that goal, effectively bringing them into our conscious awareness. This phenomenon explains why, after deciding on a particular career path or aspiration, we suddenly begin to 'see' opportunities and information related to it everywhere. The RAS doesn't create these opportunities; it simply makes us more aware of them, thereby facilitating the manifestation process.

Understanding the role of the RAS in manifestation offers a compelling insight into how our brain's natural functioning can support our efforts to achieve our career goals. However, the RAS alone does not complete the picture. The law of attraction, a theory popularised in the realm of personal development, posits that positive thoughts and energy attract positive outcomes, while negative thoughts attract negative outcomes. This principle suggests that by maintaining a positive outlook and focusing our energy on our aspirations, we can attract opportunities that align with our goals.

The law of attraction and the functioning of the RAS are interconnected. Positive thinking and visualisation can prime the RAS to notice opportunities that align with our positive expectations. This synergistic relationship between our mindset and our brain's filtering system provides a powerful framework for understanding how manifestation works. It is not merely about wishing for a desired outcome; it involves actively shaping our thought patterns and attention in ways that support the achievement of our goals.

The effectiveness of manifestation, grounded in the interplay between the RAS and the law of attraction, is further bolstered by cognitive psychology concepts such as self-efficacy and confirmation bias. Self-efficacy, the belief in one's ability to achieve goals, is a critical factor in the manifestation process. Individuals with high self-efficacy are more likely to take proactive steps towards their goals, thereby increasing the likelihood of their manifestation. Confirmation bias, the tendency to search for, interpret, and remember information in a way that confirms our preconceptions, can also play a role in manifestation by reinforcing our belief in the possibility of achieving our goals.

The principles of manifestation are not only applicable to achieving career goals but also extend to personal growth and development. The same psychological mechanisms that help us to manifest career opportunities can also facilitate personal transformation. By focusing our thoughts and energy on the person we aspire to become, we can attract experiences, relationships, and opportunities that support our growth.

Moreover, the intersection of manifestation with cognitive behavioural therapy (CBT) principles offers additional insight into its effectiveness. CBT, which focuses on changing negative thought patterns to improve mental health, shares similarities with manifestation practices. Both approaches emphasise the importance of cultivating positive thought patterns and beliefs as a way to bring about change in one's life. This alignment between psychological therapy and manifestation practices underscores the role of mindset in achieving both professional and personal objectives.

The exploration of the psychological and theoretical underpinnings of manifestation reveals a compelling narrative: our minds possess an innate ability to attract opportunities that align with our goals and aspirations. This ability, supported by the functioning of the RAS, the law of attraction, and various cognitive psychology concepts, offers a scientific basis for the practice of manifestation. It suggests that by harnessing the power of our thoughts and beliefs, we can create a reality that resonates with our deepest desires and aspirations.

As we navigate the complexities of career development and personal growth, the understanding of manifestation from a psychological perspective offers a valuable tool. It empowers us to take control of our thought patterns and focus our attention in ways that support our goals, thereby turning the seemingly intangible process of manifestation into a tangible strategy for achieving success. Through this lens, manifestation becomes not just a practice of wishful thinking, but a disciplined approach to creating the life and career we envision for ourselves.

Crafting Environments for Career Manifestation: A Harmonious Space for Aspirations

In the quest for professional fulfilment and success, the significance of aligning one's environment with career aspirations cannot be overstated. The spaces we inhabit and the company we keep do more than just influence our mood; they shape our thoughts, behaviours, and, ultimately, the trajectory of our career paths. This subtle yet profound relationship between our environment and our professional development demands a deeper exploration, as it holds the key to unlocking a level of manifestation that aligns with our deepest ambitions.

The concept of environmental alignment in the context of career manifestation is multifaceted, encompassing both the physical spaces we occupy and the social circles we immerse ourselves in. The influence of our surroundings on our professional journey is rooted in the psychological principle of priming, wherein our exposure to certain stimuli can subconsciously influence our subsequent thoughts and actions. This principle suggests that by consciously crafting our environments to reflect our career aspirations, we can prime ourselves for success and fulfilment.

Physical Environment: Crafting Spaces That Inspire and Motivate

The physical space where one works plays a crucial role in influencing productivity, creativity, and motivation. Creating a workspace that not only accommodates the practical aspects of one's work but also reflects personal career aspirations can serve as a constant source of inspiration. For instance, an individual aspiring to a career in creative writing might find inspiration in a workspace adorned with quotes from favourite authors and examples of admired works. Similarly, someone aiming for a career in architecture might surround themselves with models, sketches, and books related to their field. These environmental cues act as subtle reminders of one's goals, reinforcing commitment and focus.

Moreover, the organisation and aesthetics of a workspace can significantly impact one's mental clarity and work ethic. A cluttered desk might symbolise chaos and hinder productivity, while a neatly organised workspace can foster a sense of control and readiness. The colours, lighting, and even the presence of natural elements like plants can influence one's mood and energy levels, further affecting their ability to manifest career goals. Thus, the physical environment should not be seen merely as a backdrop to one's professional endeavours but as an active participant in their manifestation journey.

Social Environment: The Influence of Networks and Relationships

Equally influential in the manifestation of career aspirations is one's social environment. The adage 'You are the average of the five people you spend the most time with' underscores the impact of our social circles on our personal and professional development. Surrounding oneself with individuals who inspire, challenge, and support one's career aspirations can have a profound impact on one's trajectory. These relationships can provide not only emotional support and motivation but also practical assistance in the form of advice, opportunities, and resources.

Conversely, spending time in environments that are unsupportive or indifferent to one's aspirations can dampen motivation and hinder progress. It's crucial, therefore, to cultivate a network of mentors, peers, and collaborators who share or support your professional vision. Networking events, professional associations, and even social media platforms can be invaluable in connecting with like-minded individuals and fostering relationships that align with one's career aspirations.

Environmental Cues and Subconscious Influence

The power of environmental cues extends beyond the conscious mind, influencing our decisions and actions on a subconscious level. The mere presence of certain objects, images, or symbols related to one's career goals can prime the mind to pursue those goals with greater vigour. For example, a visual board displaying one's career milestones, target companies, or inspirational figures can serve as a daily reminder of one's path and purpose. These cues can trigger a cascade of thoughts and actions that align with one's aspirations, effectively programming the subconscious mind to seek out and recognise opportunities that might otherwise go unnoticed.

In addition, the language and narratives that permeate one's environment can shape their belief system and self-perception. An environment that echoes stories of success, resilience, and innovation inspires a mindset conducive to manifestation. Conversely, an environment riddled with negativity and doubt can impede one's ability to envision and pursue ambitious career goals.

Creating a Harmonious Environment for Career Manifestation

The deliberate crafting of one's physical and social environments to support their career aspirations is an art and science. It involves not only an understanding of the principles of manifestation and environmental psychology but also a deep introspection into one's desires, values, and goals. The process of aligning one's environment with their career aspirations is iterative, requiring continuous reflection and adjustment as one evolves and their career path unfolds.

This alignment is not merely about external aesthetics or social standing; it's about creating a harmonious space that resonates with one's innermost aspirations and fosters a sense of purpose, motivation, and belonging. It's about constructing a world around oneself that not only reflects where they are but also illuminates the path to where they aspire to be.

Crafting environments that support and reflect our career aspirations is a profound step towards manifesting the professional life we desire. It is an acknowledgment that our surroundings have the power to shape our thoughts, influence our actions, and, ultimately, determine the trajectory of our career paths. By aligning our environment with our aspirations, we create a fertile ground for growth, success, and fulfilment, ensuring that our professional journey is not just a pursuit of external achievements but a manifestation of our deepest values and purpose.

Chapter 2: Discovering Your Personal Purpose

In an era where the pursuit of meaning transcends the mere accumulation of professional accolades, the journey towards discovering one's personal purpose has never been more pertinent. This exploration is not just an academic exercise but a profound voyage into the depths of one's being, seeking the essence that defines and drives an individual. Personal purpose, often misconstrued as a destination, is in reality a compass, guiding us through the labyrinth of life with a sense of direction, meaning, and fulfilment.

The genesis of this journey lies in the understanding that purpose is not externally bestowed but internally discovered and cultivated. It requires a deliberate peeling away of societal layers, expectations, and oftentimes, the person we are told we ought to be, to reveal the person we truly are. This process is akin to an archaeological dig, where tools of introspection and reflection are employed to unearth the artefacts of our true desires, values, and passions.

At the heart of discovering one's personal purpose is the engagement with one's own narrative. Life is not a series of unrelated events but a tapestry woven with threads of experiences, choices, and moments of clarity. These stories we tell ourselves about who we are and what we've been through hold clues to our deeper motivations and values. Engaging with these narratives through reflective practices such as journaling or meditative introspection can illuminate patterns and themes that point towards our core essence and purpose.

Moreover, the exploration of personal purpose is deeply enriched by the cultivation of mindfulness and presence. In a world brimming with constant stimulation and distraction, the ability to be fully present with oneself is invaluable. It is in the quiet moments of solitude and stillness that we can hear the whispers of our inner voice, guiding us towards our true north. Practices that foster mindfulness, such as meditation, yoga, or simply spending time in nature, can facilitate this connection with our inner self, allowing the essence of our purpose to surface.

Another pivotal aspect of discovering personal purpose is the willingness to embrace change and uncertainty. The journey towards understanding one's purpose is rarely linear and often entails navigating through periods of ambiguity and self-doubt. These phases of uncertainty, though uncomfortable, are fertile grounds for growth and self-discovery. They challenge us to question our assumptions, to let go of what no longer serves us, and to make space for new insights and directions to emerge. The resilience and openness to evolve that this journey demands are not just by-products but integral components of discovering one's purpose.

The pursuit of personal purpose is also inherently linked to the concept of service and contribution. Purpose, in its most profound sense, transcends self-centric goals and embraces a broader vision of impact and service to others. This does not necessarily imply a grandiose scale of change but can manifest in everyday interactions, choices, and contributions that align with one's values and purpose. The intersection of personal fulfilment and positive impact on the lives of others marks a powerful convergence of purpose, where one's passions and skills meet the needs of the world.

Engaging in activities that reflect one's interests and values, seeking feedback from trusted friends or mentors, and experimenting with different roles and projects can further clarify and refine one's sense of purpose. This experiential learning approach not only deepens self-knowledge but also enhances one's ability to manifest that purpose in the world through meaningful action.

The path to discovering personal purpose is both deeply personal and universally relevant. It speaks to the core human desire for meaning, direction, and connection to something greater than oneself. While the journey is unique for each individual, the quest for purpose unites us in our shared aspiration for a life that is not just successful by external standards but deeply fulfilling and meaningful.

In essence, the discovery of personal purpose is not merely an intellectual exercise but a holistic journey that encompasses the heart, mind, and spirit. It requires curiosity, courage, and a commitment to ongoing self-exploration and growth. The reward for this journey is a life lived with intention, authenticity, and a deep sense of alignment between one's inner values and outer actions. It is, ultimately, the path to a life that resonates with the truth of who we are and the contribution we are uniquely positioned to make to the world.

The Summit of Self: Unpacking Life's Defining Moments

In the tapestry of our lives, woven with countless threads of experiences, there are those luminous strands that stand out—our peak moments. These are the times when we felt most alive, accomplished, or profoundly connected to our essence. Reflecting on these pinnacle experiences offers more than a mere stroll down memory lane; it provides invaluable insights into our core values and the essence of what brings us true satisfaction and joy. Such reflections are not merely exercises in nostalgia but pivotal explorations that can illuminate the path to discovering our personal purpose.

Each peak moment, when examined closely, is a mirror reflecting our deepest values and aspirations. These are the times when we are in full alignment with our inner selves, and the world seems to respond in kind. Whether it's the exhilaration of a professional triumph, the serenity of a connection with nature, or the warmth of a meaningful relationship, these experiences are signposts pointing towards our core values. They are the universe's way of whispering to us about what matters most in our lives.

To embark on this journey of reflection, one must first curate a mental gallery of these peak moments. Recalling these instances with as much detail as possible brings them to life in our mind's eye, allowing us to re-experience the emotions, sensations, and thoughts that accompanied them. This process is not a passive recollection but an active engagement with our past, with the aim of distilling wisdom and insight for our present and future paths.

As we delve into the essence of these peak moments, patterns begin to emerge—threads of passion, joy, and fulfilment that weave through our life's story. Perhaps it is a recurring sense of achievement in overcoming challenges, a deep satisfaction in nurturing relationships, or a profound peace in moments of solitude and reflection. These patterns are clues to our underlying values, the non-negotiable pillars upon which our sense of self is built.

Equally important is understanding the context and the elements that contributed to these peak moments. Was it the challenge and the growth it spurred? The sense of connection with others? The alignment with a cause greater than oneself? Identifying these elements not only helps in understanding what brings us joy but also in creating conditions in our present life that echo these peak experiences. It's about recreating the environment, mindset, and activities that resonate with our core values and bring out our best selves.

The act of reflecting on life's peak moments is, therefore, not a passive reminiscence but a dynamic process of self-discovery. It invites us to live our lives forward with a clearer understanding of what truly matters to us. This clarity of purpose acts as a compass, guiding our choices, actions, and aspirations towards a future that reflects our truest self.

Moreover, this reflection fosters a sense of gratitude and a positive orientation towards life. Recognising the richness of our past experiences and the values they unveil encourages a hopeful and optimistic stance towards future possibilities. It's a reaffirmation of our ability to experience joy, fulfilment, and achievement, motivating us to pursue goals and activities aligned with our essence.

Engaging in this reflective practice is a journey towards authenticity. It's about stripping away the layers of societal expectations, external pressures, and self-imposed limitations to reveal the authentic self within. This authenticity becomes the foundation upon which we build a life that is not just successful by external standards but is deeply fulfilling and meaningful.

Thus, reflecting on life's peak moments is a powerful exercise in manifesting our personal purpose. It harnesses the wisdom of our past to illuminate the path forward, guiding us towards a future where our actions, choices, and aspirations are in full alignment with our deepest values and sources of joy. It's an invitation to live a life that resonates with the truth of who we are, emboldened by the knowledge of what truly brings us satisfaction and fulfilment.

Navigating Life's Turbulence: Unearthing Purpose Through Challenges

Throughout history, the narrative of triumph over adversity has been a recurring theme, offering profound insights into the human condition and our inexorable quest for meaning. The crucible of personal challenges, often daunting in their immediacy, holds the latent power to forge clarity of purpose and resilience of spirit. This exploration delves into the transformative potential of obstacles, viewing them not as impediments but as indispensable architects of personal growth and professional destiny.

Personal challenges, in their myriad forms, serve as catalysts for introspection and self-discovery. It is through the furnace of adversity that our true strengths are refined and our deepest values brought to the fore. These periods of trial compel us to question, to reassess, and ultimately to redefine our understanding of ourselves and our place in the world. They strip away the superfluous, leaving us with the essence of who we are and what we truly value.

The journey through hardship to revelation and growth begins with the acknowledgment of our struggles. Recognising and accepting the presence of adversity is the first step towards harnessing its transformative power. This acceptance does not imply resignation but rather an openness to explore the lessons hidden within the heart of challenges. It is a stance of curiosity and courage, poised to glean wisdom from the tumult.

In navigating the terrain of personal challenges, reflection emerges as a powerful tool for uncovering hidden lessons and strengths. One effective exercise involves writing a narrative of a particularly challenging period in one's life, focusing on the emotions, thoughts, and responses it evoked. This reflective writing is not merely a recounting of events but an active search for meaning and insight. It invites the writer to consider not only what happened but also why it was significant, how it impacted their view of themselves and their world, and what strengths were discovered or developed in the process.

Another potent exercise for deriving clarity from challenges is the identification of values and beliefs that were either reinforced or re-evaluated as a result of adversity. This can be facilitated by asking oneself questions such as, "What beliefs about myself and my abilities were challenged?" and "What values did I find myself clinging to or questioning during this time?" Such inquiries encourage a deeper engagement with the internal shifts prompted by external challenges, illuminating the values and beliefs that constitute the bedrock of one's sense of purpose.

The alchemy of transformation that challenges induce is not confined to personal realms but extends into the professional domain. The competencies, insights, and resilience forged in the crucible of personal adversity are invaluable assets on the professional path. They shape our approach to work, influence our career choices, and inform our aspirations. A reflective exploration of how personal challenges have impacted one's professional journey can reveal how these experiences have directed or redirected one's career trajectory, highlighting the symbiosis between personal growth and professional development.

Moreover, the narrative of overcoming challenges is a powerful testament to one's resilience, adaptability, and strength—qualities of immense value in any professional setting. Recognising and articulating how one's experiences of adversity have cultivated these qualities can not only enhance self-understanding but also bolster one's professional identity and narrative.

The role of personal challenges in unveiling and shaping purpose is a dynamic and ongoing process. It invites a posture of lifelong learning, where each obstacle encountered is seen as an opportunity for growth, self-discovery, and clarification of purpose. This perspective transforms the narrative of adversity from one of victimhood to one of agency and empowerment.

Embracing the lessons and strengths derived from difficult times fosters a profound sense of purpose that is both resilient and responsive to life's vicissitudes. It equips us with the wisdom to navigate future challenges, the courage to pursue our aspirations, and the insight to align our professional endeavours with our deepest values and strengths.

Thus, the journey through personal challenges is not merely a path to survival but a voyage towards a deeper understanding of oneself and one's purpose. It is a process of unearthing the treasures hidden within trials, transforming adversity into opportunity, and shaping a life and career imbued with meaning, resilience, and authenticity.

Purpose with Impact: Bridging Personal Aspirations and Global Change

In an age where individual pursuits increasingly intersect with global challenges, the search for personal purpose has taken on a new dimension. The notion that one's personal mission can dovetail with broader social, environmental, or community objectives is inspiring and necessary. This alignment represents a profound shift from viewing professional success in isolation to understanding it as part of a larger impact ecosystem. This article explores aligning personal purpose with broader impact goals, offering a pathway for individuals to expand their professional aspirations to encompass contributions that resonate beyond personal achievement.

The first step in this journey involves deep introspection to articulate one's personal purpose. This process is about identifying the core values, passions, and strengths that define one's essence and drive. It is a quest to understand what moves us, what we stand for, and how we wish to express our unique talents in the world. The clarity of personal purpose serves as a compass, guiding our decisions, actions, and the impact we aspire to create.

Once a clear understanding of personal purpose is established, the next phase is to explore the broader impact goals that resonate with one's values and aspirations. This exploration requires a broadened perspective, looking beyond individual interests to consider the challenges and opportunities in our communities and the world at large. It is about asking how one's personal purpose can contribute to solving pressing societal issues, enhancing community well-being, or advocating for environmental sustainability.

To facilitate this exploration, engaging in activities that prompt reflection on the intersection between personal values and global challenges can be immensely beneficial. One such activity is the creation of a vision board that combines personal aspirations with images and words representing the broader impact goals that resonate with the individual. This visual representation can serve as a powerful reminder of the interconnectedness of personal purpose and global change.

Another activity involves conducting research to identify organisations, movements, or initiatives that align with one's personal purpose and broader impact goals. This research can reveal opportunities for collaboration, volunteering, or even career paths that bridge personal aspirations with societal contributions. It's an exercise in connecting the dots between the personal and the collective, highlighting pathways to integrate personal purpose with actions that contribute to a greater good.

Moreover, engaging in dialogue with like-minded individuals who share a commitment to making a difference can provide inspiration and new insights. Participating in forums, workshops, or networking events focused on social impact, environmental sustainability, or community development can enrich one's understanding of how personal purpose can be aligned with broader impact goals. These interactions can foster a sense of community and collaboration, reinforcing the notion that collective efforts are key to addressing global challenges.

Aligning personal purpose with broader impact goals is not a linear process but an evolving journey. It requires adaptability, continuous learning, and the courage to pursue unconventional paths. The fulfillment derived from contributing to meaningful change amplifies the sense of purpose, creating a virtuous cycle of motivation and impact.

This approach to aligning personal purpose with societal contributions represents a paradigm shift in defining success. It reframes professional aspirations to include not only personal achievement but also the positive imprint we leave on the world. It is an invitation to embark on a fulfilling journey that combines personal fulfilment with meaningful impact, embodying the principle that true success is measured not just by what we accomplish for ourselves but by the difference we make in the lives of others and the health of our planet.

Thus, the pursuit of aligning personal purpose with broader impact goals is more than a professional aspiration; it is a commitment to a way of life. It challenges us to think deeply about the legacy we wish to leave and the world we want to help shape. It is a powerful expression of our humanity, a testament to our capacity to envision and enact change, grounding our personal pursuits in a broader context of global responsibility and shared destiny.

Exercises to Clarify Your Values, Passions, and Purpose

In the journey of self-discovery, understanding one's personal values, passions, and purpose serves as the north star, guiding decisions, shaping goals, and providing a sense of direction. The quest for clarity in these areas can be both challenging and profoundly rewarding. It demands introspection, honesty, and a willingness to engage deeply with one's inner world. This article presents a series of exercises designed to illuminate the path to discovering your personal values, igniting your passions, and articulating your purpose.

1. Values Mapping

Your values are the principles that matter most to you, acting as the bedrock of your personal and professional life. To identify these, begin with a values mapping exercise.

- Start by listing out values that resonate with you. These could range from creativity, integrity, and compassion, to innovation, freedom, and leadership.

- Once you have a comprehensive list, narrow it down to your top five values. Ask yourself, "Which of these values am I unwilling to compromise on?"

- For each of the top five values, write a brief narrative explaining why this value is important to you and how you've lived it out in your life. This narrative reinforces your connection to each value and clarifies its role in your life.

2. Passion Projects

Passions are the activities, interests, or ideas that deeply engage you and bring you joy. Identifying your passions can lead you to a purposeful path.

- Reflect on moments when you lost track of time or felt completely absorbed in an activity. What were you doing?

- Write about a project or activity where you felt most alive and fulfilled. This could be anything from a hobby, a side project, a volunteer experience, or even a course you took.

- Analyze these experiences to uncover common themes. Is there a particular cause, activity, or subject matter that consistently ignites your passion?

3. Purpose Statement Crafting

Your purpose is your reason for being, the unique imprint you wish to leave on the world. Crafting a purpose statement synthesizes your values and passions into a coherent vision.

- Reflect on the intersection of your top values and passions. Ask yourself, "How can I use my passions to live out my values?"

- Consider the impact you want to have. Who do you want to help? What change do you wish to see in the world?

- Write a draft of your purpose statement. Keep it concise, aiming for one or two sentences that encapsulate your essence and aspiration. For example, "My purpose is to use my creativity and compassion to inspire and empower others to achieve their full potential."

4. Vision Board Creation

A vision board is a visual representation of your values, passions, and purpose, serving as a constant reminder and source of inspiration.

- Gather magazines, photos, quotes, and any other items that resonate with your identified values and passions.

- Assemble these items on a board or digital platform in a way that visually represents your purpose and aspirations.

- Place your vision board somewhere you will see it daily to keep your values, passions, and purpose at the forefront of your mind.

5. Reflective Journaling

Journaling is a powerful tool for self-reflection and clarity. Use it as a daily practice to explore your thoughts and feelings about your values, passions, and purpose.

- Dedicate time each day to write freely about your experiences living out your values, engaging in your passions, and pursuing your purpose.

- Reflect on any challenges or successes you encounter and what they reveal about your path to purpose.

- Use journal prompts such as, "What did I do today that felt meaningful?" or "How did I live out one of my top values today?"

Engaging in these exercises is an ongoing process, not a one-time event. Your values, passions, and purpose may evolve over time, and revisiting these exercises periodically can provide continuous clarity and direction. By investing time and effort into clarifying these essential aspects of your identity, you pave the way for a life lived with intention, fulfilment, and alignment with your truest self.

Chapter 3: Setting Intentional Career Goals

Embarking on a career path without clear goals is akin to navigating a vast ocean without a compass. As we delve into the heart of manifesting a career that resonates with our deepest aspirations, the importance of setting intentional career goals becomes unequivocally clear. This chapter is dedicated to transforming the abstract into the tangible, guiding you through the process of defining, refining, and achieving career goals that are not only ambitious but deeply aligned with your personal values and ultimate purpose.

The journey of setting intentional career goals is both an art and a science. It requires a delicate balance between dreaming big and grounding those dreams in actionable plans. This chapter will explore the nuanced difference between goals and intentions, illuminating how intentions can breathe life and direction into your goals, making them more meaningful and attainable.

We will introduce you to the SMART criteria—a time-tested method that ensures your career goals are Specific, Measurable, Achievable, Relevant, and Time-bound. But beyond the mechanics of goal-setting, we will delve into the power of visualization, a potent tool in your goal-setting arsenal that enables you to see, feel, and experience your success even before it materializes.

Aligning your career goals with your personal values and purpose is crucial. A career that is not in harmony with your inner self is unlikely to bring the fulfillment you seek. Therefore, this chapter will provide strategies for ensuring that your career aspirations are a true reflection of who you are and what you wish to contribute to the world.

Breaking down your overarching career goals into actionable steps is essential for progress. We will guide you through this process, helping you transform your vision into a series of manageable actions that will lead you closer to your dream career with each step you take.

Setting up a goal achievement plan is pivotal in the journey towards career manifestation. This chapter will equip you with the tools to create a comprehensive plan, including how to set milestones, anticipate challenges, and devise strategies to overcome them. Accountability plays a significant role in achieving your career goals, and we will discuss how leveraging external support can magnify your success.

However, the path to achieving your career goals is not static. As your career evolves, so too will your goals. We will explore the importance of adaptability in goal setting, offering insights on how to pivot gracefully and effectively when the need arises.

Incorporating continuous learning and growth into your career goals ensures that you are not just achieving but also evolving. We will highlight ways to embrace lifelong learning as a key component of your career development.

Finally, we will stress the importance of celebrating milestones and reflecting on your journey. Recognizing your progress not only boosts your motivation but also provides valuable insights into your strengths, areas for improvement, and the resilience you possess.

Setting intentional career goals is a journey of discovery, growth, and fulfillment. As you turn the pages of this chapter, you will be equipped with the knowledge and tools to set career goals that not only propel you towards professional success but also ensure a career that is rich in purpose and personal satisfaction. Let us embark on this journey together, charting a course towards a future where your career is not just a job, but a reflection of your deepest values and aspirations.

Goals vs. Intentions: Crafting a Blueprint for Purposeful Success

In the landscape of personal and professional development, the concepts of goals and intentions often intertwine, yet they hold distinct meanings and serve different purposes. Understanding the nuanced differences between the two can significantly enhance one's journey towards a more fulfilling and purpose-driven life. This exploration seeks to unravel the threads that distinguish goals from intentions, shedding light on how a harmonious blend of both elements can sculpt a path to meaningful achievement and inner satisfaction.

Goals are the milestones we set on our journey, concrete objectives we aim to achieve within a specific timeframe. They are the targets we set in our sights, quantifiable and often tangible achievements that serve as benchmarks for our progress. Goals are the answer to the "what" and "when" of our aspirations, providing a clear direction and a sense of focus. They are the manifestation of our ambition, encapsulated in measurable outcomes such as earning a degree, securing a job promotion, or running a marathon.

Intentions, however, operate on a subtler level. They are the undercurrents that guide our journey, rooted in our values, beliefs, and the essence of who we strive to be. Intentions answer the "why" and "how" of our pursuits, reflecting the mindset and the values that propel us forward. They are less about achieving a specific outcome and more about the quality of the journey, the person we become in the process of striving towards our goals. Intentions are grounded in the present, focusing on the attitudes, values, and behaviours that we bring to each day and each task before us.

The distinction between goals and intentions can be likened to the relationship between a destination and the compass that guides us there. While goals provide a destination to aim for, intentions offer the moral and ethical compass that steers our course. Goals compel us to look ahead to future achievements, whereas intentions draw our attention to the present, to the immediate choices and actions that define our path.

Integrating goals and intentions in our career planning and personal development can lead to a richer, more rewarding journey. Setting goals without the foundation of clear intentions may lead to success that feels hollow or achievements that drift away from our core values. Conversely, cultivating intentions without setting specific goals may result in a lack of direction and tangible progress. The magic lies in the synergy of both elements, where goals give form to our aspirations, and intentions infuse those aspirations with depth and meaning.

To navigate this integration effectively, one might begin by articulating clear, specific goals that resonate with their aspirations. Following this, a reflective exploration of the intentions behind these goals can enrich the process. Questions such as, "Why is this goal important to me?" and "How does pursuing this goal reflect my values and beliefs?" can help clarify the intentions that underpin our objectives. This introspective process ensures that our goals are not just ladders to external success but bridges to personal growth and self-realization.

Practical exercises can further this integration. For instance, for each goal, individuals could write down the values and intentions that align with it, creating a manifesto that combines the "what" with the "why" and "how". Visualisation techniques, imagining not only the achievement of the goal but also embodying the intended values and attitudes, can solidify this connection, making the pursuit more holistic and aligned.

Moreover, regularly revisiting and reflecting on both goals and intentions can ensure they remain in harmony. Life's inevitable changes and personal growth may shift our perspectives, requiring adjustments to ensure our goals and intentions continue to resonate with our evolving self.

In essence, the confluence of goals and intentions paves the way for a holistic approach to achievement, one that values the end as much as the means. It recognises that true success is not measured by the accumulation of achievements but by how those achievements reflect our deepest values and aspirations. By embracing both goals and intentions, we chart a course towards not only achieving what we set out to do but also becoming who we wish to be in the process. This dual focus transforms the journey towards personal and professional development into an enriching voyage of discovery, where each achievement is a step towards realising our fullest potential, guided by the true north of our intentions.

Sculpting Success: The Art of SMART Career Goal Setting

In the dynamic realm of career development, the creation of clear, actionable goals is not just beneficial; it's imperative for progress and success. Goals provide a roadmap, directing efforts and resources towards meaningful outcomes. However, not all goals are created equal. The effectiveness of a goal largely depends on its structure and specificity. Enter the SMART framework, a beacon for individuals navigating the often-turbulent waters of career advancement. This article delves into the art of crafting career goals through the SMART lens—Specific, Measurable, Achievable, Relevant, and Time-bound—offering a blueprint for those aspiring to elevate their professional trajectory.

Specificity: The Keystone of Goal Setting

The foundation of any effective goal is specificity. Vague aspirations, such as "I want to be successful in my career," lack the clarity necessary for actionable steps. Specificity transforms these nebulous desires into tangible objectives. For instance, "I aim to secure a role as a Marketing Manager at a leading tech company within the next two years" pinpoints the what, where, and when, providing a clear direction for your efforts.

Measurability: The Scale of Progress

A goal without a measure of success is like a journey without a destination. Measurability allows for the tracking of progress and the celebration of milestones along the way. It answers the question, "How will I know when I have achieved my goal?" If your goal is to ascend to a managerial position, a measurable indicator could be the acquisition of specific leadership skills or responsibilities, quantified by leadership courses completed or projects led.

Achievability: The Realm of Realism

While ambition is a commendable trait, a goal must reside within the realm of achievability to motivate rather than demoralise. This aspect of the SMART criteria assesses the feasibility of the goal given current resources, constraints, and skills. It encourages a realistic appraisal of what's possible, prompting consideration of the steps necessary to bridge the gap between current reality and the desired future. For example, if you aspire to a role that typically requires a higher level of education, determining the achievability of your goal might involve planning for further study.

Relevance: The Alignment with Aspirations

Relevance ensures that your goal is aligned with your broader career aspirations and values. It anchors your goal within the larger context of your professional vision, ensuring that each step forward is not just a move towards a specific objective but towards the fulfillment of your personal mission. A goal to transition into a new industry, for example, should reflect a genuine interest and alignment with your long-term career aspirations, such as a passion for renewable energy if you're aiming to move into the green tech sector.

Time-bound: The Importance of Deadlines

A deadline acts as a catalyst, converting intention into action. Setting a timeframe establishes a sense of urgency, keeping procrastination at bay and maintaining momentum. Whether it's six months to master a new software relevant to your field or one year to land a new job, a deadline can compartmentalise the journey, making the goal more digestible and less daunting.

Applying the SMART Framework: A Practical Example

Consider the goal of "improving networking skills to advance my career." Through the SMART lens, this could be refined to: "Within the next three months, I will attend at least four industry networking events and connect with a minimum of 20 professionals in my field to enhance my networking skills and identify new career opportunities."

This example embodies the SMART criteria by specifying the action (attending networking events, connecting with professionals), measuring success (four events, 20 connections), ensuring achievability (selecting accessible events), confirming relevance (advancing career opportunities), and setting a time limit (three months).

Crafting SMART Career Goals: The Journey Ahead

The journey of career development is punctuated with aspirations and ambitions, each requiring careful planning and execution. The SMART framework offers a systematic approach to transforming these dreams into achievable milestones. By setting goals that are Specific, Measurable, Achievable, Relevant, and Time-bound, you equip yourself with a powerful toolkit for career advancement. This methodical approach not only streamlines the path towards your objectives but also instils a sense of purpose and direction in your professional journey. As you apply the SMART criteria to your career aspirations, remember that each goal set is a step towards not just professional achievement, but personal fulfillment and growth.

Crafting Your Career Goal Achievement Plan

In the quest for career advancement, setting goals is merely the first step; the crux of success lies in crafting a meticulous plan for achieving these goals. A well-thought-out goal achievement plan is akin to a map in the hands of a traveller; it provides direction, anticipates challenges, and suggests alternate routes to ensure the journey is fruitful and the destination, attainable. This article endeavours to guide you through the development of a comprehensive plan that not only delineates your career goals but also lays down a structured approach to achieving them, identifying potential obstacles along the way, and devising strategies to navigate through them.

Charting the Course: Setting Milestones

The journey towards any significant career goal can seem daunting when viewed in its entirety. Breaking down this journey into smaller, more manageable segments by setting milestones is a pivotal first step. Milestones serve as checkpoints along your path, offering opportunities to assess progress, recalibrate strategies, and celebrate small victories. For instance, if your goal is to transition into a leadership role within your organisation, milestones could include completing specific leadership training, leading a project team, or receiving a certain amount of positive feedback from peers and supervisors. Each milestone achieved is a step closer to your overarching goal, providing momentum and a sense of accomplishment.

Foreseeing Challenges: Identifying Potential Obstacles

Every journey encounters its share of obstacles, and the path to your career goals will be no different. Anticipating these challenges in advance can equip you with the foresight to navigate through them effectively when they arise. Begin by conducting a thorough analysis of your goal, considering internal factors such as skill gaps or limiting beliefs, and external factors like market conditions or organisational constraints. Acknowledging these potential roadblocks early on allows you to approach your goal with a realistic outlook, setting the stage for strategic problem-solving down the line.

Strategising Success: Overcoming Obstacles

Identifying potential obstacles is only half the battle; the key to a robust goal achievement plan lies in formulating strategies to overcome these hurdles. This involves a dual approach: proactive prevention and reactive resolution. Proactive prevention aims to minimise the impact of foreseeable challenges through planning and preparation. For example, if a skill gap is identified as a potential obstacle, enrolling in relevant courses or seeking mentorship can be effective strategies to bridge this gap before it becomes a hindrance.

Reactive resolution, on the other hand, focuses on developing a flexible mindset and adaptable strategies to address obstacles as they arise. This could involve seeking feedback and advice, leveraging your network for support, or even revisiting and adjusting your milestones as necessary. The essence of overcoming obstacles lies in resilience and adaptability; the ability to stay committed to your goal, irrespective of the challenges encountered.

Navigating the Path: Leveraging Resources and Support

No goal is achieved in isolation. Identifying and leveraging available resources and support systems can significantly enhance your chances of success. This includes tangible resources such as educational materials, financial support, and technology, as well as intangible resources like professional networks, mentors, and peer support. Actively seek out individuals who have navigated similar paths and learn from their experiences. Surrounding yourself with a supportive community not only provides valuable insights and guidance but also keeps you motivated and accountable to your goals.

Reflecting and Reassessing: The Importance of Regular Review

A goal achievement plan is not set in stone; it is a living document that should evolve as you progress towards your goals. Regularly reviewing your plan allows you to assess what is working and what isn't, providing an opportunity to adjust your strategies, refine your milestones, and even reassess your goals if necessary. This iterative process is crucial for maintaining relevance and ensuring that your plan remains aligned with your changing aspirations, circumstances, and the external environment.

Developing a comprehensive plan for achieving your career goals is an exercise in foresight, strategy, and adaptability. It requires you to set clear milestones, anticipate and prepare for potential obstacles, and leverage available resources and support. Equally important is the willingness to reassess and adjust your plan as you gather insights and experience along your journey. Remember, the ultimate purpose of this plan is not merely to achieve specific career milestones but to navigate the path towards these milestones with intention, learning, and growth. As you embark on this journey, armed with a detailed blueprint for success, each step taken is a testament to your commitment to personal and professional development, leading you closer to the fulfillment of your career aspirations.

Transforming Career Goals into Actionable Pathways

In the journey of career advancement, the vision of one's ultimate goal often looms large, a towering summit in the distance. While the end point might sparkle with promise, the path towards it can seem daunting, a landscape filled with uncertainties and challenges. The art of breaking down overarching career goals into smaller, manageable actions is akin to mapping out the route to this summit, transforming a distant dream into a series of achievable steps. This article explores strategies for deconstructing career goals, providing a framework that empowers individuals to navigate their career trajectory with confidence and clarity.

The Art of Decomposition

The first step in making your career goals more approachable is to deconstruct them into smaller objectives. This process, known as decomposition, involves dividing a large goal into sub-goals that are more immediate and achievable. For instance, if your overarching goal is to become a senior manager in your field, your sub-goals might include developing specific leadership skills, expanding your professional network, and gaining experience in project management. This segmentation not only makes the goal seem more attainable but also provides clear directions for your efforts.

Defining Actionable Steps

Once you have identified your sub-goals, the next step is to outline actionable steps for each. Actionable steps are specific tasks or activities that move you closer to achieving your sub-goals. For each sub-goal, ask yourself, "What actions can I take right now to make progress?" These actions should be clear and precise, such as completing a leadership training course, attending networking events, or volunteering to lead a small project at work. The specificity of these steps is crucial, as it translates abstract aspirations into concrete tasks.

Prioritising and Scheduling

With a list of actionable steps in hand, prioritising and scheduling become key. Not all actions carry the same weight towards achieving your sub-goals, and not all need to be executed immediately. Evaluate the impact and urgency of each step to determine its priority. This assessment allows you to focus on activities that offer the most significant leverage towards your goals. Subsequently, incorporate these steps into your daily or weekly schedule, ensuring that you allocate time and resources efficiently. This structured approach prevents overwhelm and keeps you focused on progressing methodically towards your objectives.

Monitoring Progress and Adjusting Course

As you embark on the execution of your actionable steps, it is vital to monitor your progress and remain flexible. The path towards your career goals is rarely linear, and you may encounter unexpected challenges or opportunities that necessitate adjustments to your plan. Regularly reviewing your progress against your sub-goals and actionable steps allows you to adapt your strategies, refine your approach, and, if necessary, redefine your objectives. This iterative process is essential for staying aligned with your evolving aspirations and the dynamic nature of career development.

Celebrating Milestones

Recognising and celebrating each milestone achieved on your journey is crucial for maintaining motivation. The completion of actionable steps and the attainment of sub-goals are achievements in their own right, marking your progress towards the larger objective. Acknowledge these successes, however small they may seem, and allow yourself to savour the satisfaction of moving closer to your career summit. These celebrations serve as reminders of your capability and resilience, fuelling your journey forward.

Leveraging Support Systems

No journey is undertaken in isolation, and the path towards your career goals is no exception. Engage with mentors, peers, and professional networks for support, advice, and encouragement. Sharing your goals and the steps you're taking to achieve them can open doors to resources, opportunities, and invaluable insights. Additionally, accountability partnerships can provide the motivation and discipline required to stay on track, making the journey more collaborative and enriching.

The strategy of breaking down career goals into actionable steps demystifies the process of career advancement, transforming lofty aspirations into a structured path of tangible progress. By decomposing goals, defining actionable steps, and integrating these into a prioritised and flexible plan, individuals can navigate their career trajectory with a sense of empowerment and control. Through regular reflection, celebration of achievements, and engagement with supportive communities, the journey towards career fulfilment becomes not just feasible, but deeply rewarding. In mastering the mosaic of career development, every step taken is a piece placed in the larger picture of one's professional legacy, a testament to the power of intention, action, and persistence.

Mastering the Art of Career Evolution

In the world of professional development, the path of a career is seldom a straight line. The landscape of work, influenced by technological advances, economic shifts, and personal growth, demands not just steadfast ambition but a nimble adaptability. The capacity to refine and sometimes radically alter career goals in response to evolving circumstances is not a sign of indecision but a strategic imperative for sustained relevance and fulfillment. This exploration seeks to illuminate the necessity of flexibility in goal setting, offering insights on navigating the fluid dynamics of career progression while staying true to one's foundational values and overarching purpose.

The Nature of Change

Change is the only constant in the professional realm. Industries evolve, new roles emerge, and personal interests and values mature over time. This evolution is not merely external; it prompts a corresponding shift within individuals, urging a reassessment of what one seeks from a career. Recognising and embracing this flux is the first step towards mastering the art of career adaptability. It involves cultivating an openness to new experiences and a willingness to question and redefine one's career aspirations as part of ongoing personal and professional growth.

Strategies for Adaptable Goal Setting

Adapting career goals in the face of change requires more than just flexibility; it demands a strategic approach grounded in self-awareness and foresight. Herein lies a blueprint for navigating this adaptive process:

1. Regular Reflection and Re-evaluation

Institute a practice of periodic self-reflection, assessing the alignment of your career goals with your current interests, skills, and the market landscape. This can involve setting aside time for a thorough review of your career plan at regular intervals, questioning not just the viability of your goals but their resonance with your evolving self.

2. Cultivating a Learning Mindset

Embrace a philosophy of lifelong learning, recognising that the acquisition of new skills and knowledge is not just a means to an end but an integral part of career adaptability. This mindset enables you to pivot more easily, as it expands your horizons and equips you with a broader toolkit for navigating change.

3. Building a Diverse Network

Cultivate a wide-ranging professional network that extends beyond your current industry or role. Diverse connections provide insights into different sectors, new technologies, and emerging trends, offering inspiration for potential career pivots and the support system necessary to navigate them.

4. Scenario Planning

Engage in scenario planning, envisaging various career paths and the steps needed to pivot towards them. This involves considering different career scenarios, evaluating their alignment with your values and purpose, and mapping out the actionable steps required to transition from one path to another.

5. Embracing Experimentation

Adopt an experimental approach to your career, viewing each role, project, and even setback as an opportunity to learn and refine your career aspirations. This perspective encourages a proactive engagement with change, transforming the fear of the unknown into a curiosity-driven exploration.

6. Flexibility in Goal Setting

Incorporate flexibility into your goal-setting process, establishing goals that are specific and ambitious yet allow for adjustment. This might mean setting broader objectives that can accommodate shifts in direction or breaking down goals into shorter-term milestones that can be adapted as circumstances evolve.

Staying Anchored in Values and Purpose

Amid the flux of career evolution, your values and purpose serve as your compass, ensuring that adaptations in your career trajectory do not lead you astray from what fundamentally matters to you. Revisiting and reaffirming these core principles during times of change ensures that your career pivots are not just reactive responses to external pressures but deliberate choices that enhance your professional satisfaction and personal growth.

Navigating Transition

Navigating career transitions, especially significant pivots, requires courage, resilience, and strategic planning. It involves assessing the gaps between your current position and your new direction, identifying the skills, experiences, and connections needed to bridge these gaps, and systematically pursuing these prerequisites. Support from mentors, career coaches, or peer groups can provide valuable guidance and encouragement during this transformative phase.

The agile path of career development is not for the faint-hearted. It challenges conventional notions of linear progression, demanding instead a dynamic engagement with the ebbs and flows of professional life. Adapting career goals as circumstances evolve is a profound exercise in self-discovery, resilience, and strategic planning. It requires a balance between ambition and adaptability, foresight and flexibility, ensuring that each pivot not only advances your career but enriches your professional journey with depth, diversity, and fulfillment. In mastering the art of career evolution, you learn that true success lies not in the unwavering pursuit of predefined goals but in the ability to navigate change with grace, purpose, and an unwavering commitment to personal growth.

Embracing the Infinite Climb

In the dynamic expanse of modern career landscapes, the pursuit of success transcends the boundaries of mere job performance. It ventures into the realms of continuous learning and personal development, areas that have become indispensable for professionals aiming to not only navigate but also thrive in the complexities of today's professional world. This article delves into the essence of lifelong learning and personal growth, illustrating their pivotal role in career advancement and offering insights into integrating continuous improvement into one's professional journey.

The Imperative of Lifelong Learning

The velocity of change in technology, industry trends, and job markets today is unparalleled. In this context, the concept of lifelong learning emerges not as a choice but as a necessity for anyone aspiring to maintain relevance and excellence in their professional endeavours. Lifelong learning encompasses the ongoing, voluntary, and self-motivated pursuit of knowledge, whether for personal or professional reasons. It is the acknowledgment that the end of formal education is not the end of one's educational journey but merely a beginning.

The Multifaceted Benefits of Continuous Learning

Engaging in continuous learning offers a multitude of benefits, extending beyond the acquisition of new skills and knowledge. It fosters adaptability, a critical attribute in a constantly evolving job market, enabling professionals to pivot seamlessly across roles and industries. Moreover, it cultivates a mindset of curiosity and openness, encouraging innovation and creative problem-solving. Perhaps most importantly, lifelong learning contributes to personal fulfillment, providing a sense of achievement and purpose that transcends occupational success.

Strategies for Integrating Learning into Career Development

1. **Personal Development Plans**: Crafting a personal development plan is a strategic approach to integrating learning into your career. Begin by assessing your current skills and identifying gaps relative to your career aspirations. Set learning goals that address these gaps, and outline specific actions, resources, and timelines for achieving them.

2. **Leveraging Online Learning Platforms**: The digital age offers an abundance of resources for self-improvement. Online platforms such as Coursera, LinkedIn Learning, and Udemy provide access to courses across a wide range of subjects, offering flexibility to learn at one's own pace and convenience. Engaging with these resources can provide valuable skills and certifications that enhance your professional profile.

3. **Industry Networking and Professional Associations**: Active participation in professional associations and networking groups can be a rich source of learning. These forums offer insights into industry trends, best practices, and emerging challenges, facilitating informal learning through discussions, seminars, and workshops.

4. **Mentorship and Coaching**: Seeking mentorship or engaging with a career coach can significantly accelerate personal growth. Mentors provide guidance, feedback, and advice based on their experiences, offering a personalised learning experience that can help navigate career challenges and opportunities more effectively.

5. **Reflective Practices**: Incorporating reflective practices such as journaling or meditation into your routine can

enhance self-awareness and personal development. Reflection allows for the consolidation of learning, helping to internalise lessons from experiences and apply them in future contexts.

6. **Cross-functional Projects and Job Rotation**: Volunteering for projects outside your immediate role or pursuing job rotation opportunities within your organisation can expose you to new challenges and learning opportunities. These experiences broaden your skill set and provide a deeper understanding of different aspects of your industry or company.

Navigating Obstacles to Continuous Learning

Despite its benefits, integrating continuous learning into one's career is not without challenges. Time constraints, financial considerations, and at times, lack of institutional support can impede learning efforts. Overcoming these obstacles requires creativity and commitment. This might involve allocating specific times for learning, exploring free or subsidised learning resources, or discussing professional development opportunities with employers.

The Unending Journey

The journey of lifelong learning and personal development is unending, an infinite climb towards personal and professional excellence. It is a journey marked by curiosity, resilience, and the pursuit of purpose. Embracing this journey can transform the trajectory of your career, opening doors to new possibilities and ensuring that you remain not just competitive but fulfilled and inspired by your professional life.

In essence, incorporating continuous learning and growth into your career is not merely a strategy for advancement but a manifesto for a rich, evolving professional identity. It invites an ongoing engagement with the world of knowledge, ensuring that as the professional landscape evolves, so too do you, equipped not only with the skills of today but with the adaptive prowess to embrace the unknown challenges of tomorrow.

Chapter 4: Overcoming Obstacles and Mindset Shifts

The journey towards career fulfilment and success is rarely a straight path devoid of hurdles. Instead, it is often a winding road, fraught with obstacles that test our resilience, adaptability, and conviction. From external challenges such as industry downturns and technological disruptions to internal battles with imposter syndrome and fear of failure, these obstacles can seem insurmountable, potentially derailing even the most meticulously planned career trajectories. However, it is precisely in navigating these challenges that profound growth and self-discovery occur. "Overcoming Obstacles and Mindset Shifts" delves into the heart of these challenges, unveiling the transformative power of resilience and the pivotal role of mindset in transcending professional hurdles.

This chapter is dedicated to unraveling the complex tapestry of career obstacles, illuminating the strategies, psychological insights, and mindset adjustments necessary to turn these challenges into catalysts for growth and success. It acknowledges the universality of career obstacles, providing a beacon of hope and a toolkit for those who find themselves in the throes of professional adversity. Here, we explore not only the nature of these challenges but also the foundational shifts in perspective that transform obstacles from barriers to stepping stones.

Understanding that the key to overcoming obstacles often lies in our perception and response, this chapter introduces the concept of mindset shifts—fundamental changes in how we view ourselves and our career paths. By embracing a growth mindset, we open ourselves to learning, resilience, and a proactive approach to challenges. This mindset empowers us to view failure not as a verdict on our capabilities but as a valuable learning experience, a necessary detour on the path to achievement.

We venture into the realm of resilience, unpacking the psychological and emotional fortitude that allows us to withstand and emerge stronger from career setbacks. Resilience is not an innate trait but a skill that can be cultivated through mindful practices, supportive relationships, and an unwavering commitment to our personal and professional growth.

This chapter also offers practical strategies and exercises designed to fortify your resilience, shift your mindset, and navigate the inevitable obstacles that arise on the journey toward career fulfilment. From building a robust support network to mastering the art of constructive reflection on failures, these strategies are geared towards fostering a resilient, growth-oriented approach to your career.

As we traverse the landscape of "Overcoming Obstacles and Mindset Shifts," we invite you to engage with this chapter not just as a reader but as an active participant in your own story of professional development. The insights and tools shared here are intended to guide you through the process of transforming obstacles into opportunities, fear into fortitude, and challenges into chapters of your unique narrative of success.

In this journey of overcoming and growth, remember that the most formidable obstacles often precede the greatest breakthroughs. Armed with resilience, a growth mindset, and a suite of strategies for navigating professional hurdles, you are well-equipped to turn the challenges you face into the foundations upon which your career success is built.

Understanding Career Obstacles

The pathway to professional accomplishment is often littered with an array of obstacles that can hinder progress, induce stress, and, at times, lead to a complete reevaluation of career goals. These hurdles are not merely impediments but essential elements of the career journey, offering opportunities for growth, learning, and self-reflection. Understanding the nature of these challenges is the first step towards developing effective strategies for overcoming them. This exploration delves into the myriad obstacles professionals encounter along their career path, ranging from internal psychological battles to external economic and sector-specific upheavals.

The Spectre of Failure

Perhaps the most pervasive fear that professionals face is the fear of failure. This apprehension can stifle innovation, deter risk-taking, and limit career advancement. It stems from a deep-seated aversion to the prospect of not meeting expectations—be they personal, societal, or professional. The fear of failure often leads to a paralysis of action, where the dread of potential negative outcomes outweighs the desire to pursue ambitious goals.

Battling Imposter Syndrome

Closely linked to the fear of failure is imposter syndrome, a psychological phenomenon where individuals doubt their accomplishments and fear being exposed as a "fraud." This can be particularly debilitating in environments that prize competence and achievement, leading professionals to undervalue their contributions and capabilities. Imposter syndrome sows seeds of self-doubt, hindering individuals from fully embracing and capitalising on opportunities for growth and advancement.

The Challenge of Directionlessness

A lack of clear direction can also significantly impede career progression. Professionals, especially those in the early stages of their career or those contemplating a transition, may find themselves at a crossroads, unsure of which path to pursue. This uncertainty can lead to stagnation, as individuals struggle to make decisions that align with their long-term objectives and personal values.

External Forces and Economic Shifts

Beyond the internal psychological barriers lie external obstacles, including economic downturns, industry shifts, and technological disruptions. These factors can render certain skills obsolete, necessitate rapid adaptation, and even lead to job loss. Navigating these tumultuous waters requires a keen understanding of market trends, a willingness to upskill or reskill, and, crucially, the flexibility to pivot towards new opportunities.

Overcoming These Hurdles

Overcoming these career obstacles necessitates a multifaceted approach. Confronting the fear of failure involves reframing failure as an integral part of the learning process—a stepping stone rather than a stumbling block. It requires cultivating resilience and developing a tolerance for ambiguity and uncertainty.

Addressing imposter syndrome calls for a reinforcement of self-worth and the acknowledgment of one's achievements. This can be facilitated through mentorship, feedback, and a conscious effort to internalise successes rather than attribute them to external factors.

Navigating a lack of direction benefits from introspection and exploration. Setting aside time to reflect on personal values, interests, and long-term goals can clarify one's career aspirations. Experimentation, through job shadowing, informational interviews, or short-term projects, can also offer insights into potential career paths.

In response to external challenges such as economic shifts and industry disruptions, professionals must embrace continuous learning and adaptability. Staying abreast of industry trends, investing in lifelong learning, and cultivating a network of contacts across different sectors can enhance one's ability to adapt to changing circumstances.

The Way Forward

Understanding and navigating career obstacles is an integral part of professional development. Each hurdle encountered presents an opportunity to build resilience, acquire new knowledge, and refine one's career trajectory. By adopting a proactive and reflective approach to these challenges, professionals can not only overcome them but emerge stronger, more adaptable, and more aligned with their core values and career aspirations.

In essence, the journey through professional quagmires is not one to be undertaken alone. Seeking support, fostering connections, and engaging in continuous self-improvement are pivotal in navigating the complex landscape of career development. As professionals, embracing these obstacles as opportunities for growth enables us to chart a course through the uncertain waters of our career paths, guided by the stars of our aspirations and the compass of our values.

Unravelling the Psychology of Resilience

In the intricate dance of career progression, resilience emerges not just as a desirable attribute but as an indispensable force. It is the mental toughness and flexibility that empowers individuals to navigate through, and bounce back from, the inevitable setbacks and challenges that mar the professional landscape. This exploration delves into the psychological underpinnings of resilience, shedding light on how it can be cultivated to foster a robustness that ensures not merely survival but thriving in the face of career adversities.

Resilience, in its essence, is the amalgamation of psychological stamina and emotional agility. It is the dynamic process through which individuals exhibit positive adaptation despite experiencing significant sources of stress or trauma. The roots of resilience can be traced to a combination of intrinsic personal traits and extrinsic support systems, intertwined with learned behaviors and thought patterns. It is a misconception that resilience is a trait that individuals either possess or lack; rather, it is a skill set that can be developed and enhanced over time.

The Bedrock of Resilience: Understanding its Components

The psychology of resilience is supported by several key components, each contributing to the overall capacity to withstand pressures and rebound from setbacks. These include self-efficacy, optimism, flexibility, and social support, amongst others.

Self-efficacy, or the belief in one's own ability to overcome challenges and achieve goals, stands as a cornerstone of resilience. This confidence, rooted in past successes and a realistic appraisal of one's capabilities, fuels persistence and effort in the face of difficulties.

Optimism, characterised by a positive yet realistic outlook on life, enables resilient individuals to maintain hope and see setbacks as temporary and surmountable. This perspective encourages a proactive approach to problem-solving and mitigates the risk of falling into despair.

Flexibility, or the capacity to adapt to changing circumstances and alter strategies when faced with obstacles, is critical. It embodies the understanding that rigidity often leads to breakage, while adaptability fosters growth and learning.

Social support plays a pivotal role in resilience, offering a buffer against the impacts of stress and adversity. Strong, positive relationships provide emotional sustenance, practical assistance, and a sense of belonging and value.

Cultivating Resilience: Strategies for Strengthening Psychological Fortitude

Developing resilience is akin to building muscle; it requires consistent effort, practice, and the right strategies. Here are some approaches to fostering resilience:

1. Embrace Challenge as Opportunity: Reconceptualise challenges as opportunities for growth rather than insurmountable obstacles. This shift in perspective encourages engagement with difficulties, fostering learning and development.

2. Cultivate a Growth Mindset: Adopt the belief that abilities and intelligence can be developed through dedication and hard work. This mindset embraces failure as a necessary part of the learning process, encouraging perseverance.

3. Build Emotional Awareness: Enhance emotional intelligence by becoming more aware of, and comfortable with, a wide range of emotions. This awareness allows for better management of stress and adversity.

4. Foster Strong Relationships: Invest in building and maintaining supportive relationships. This network becomes a critical resource during times of stress, providing emotional support and practical assistance.

5. Practice Self-Care: Regularly engage in activities that promote physical, emotional, and mental well-being. Self-care acts as a foundation for resilience, enabling individuals to operate from a place of strength.

6. Develop Problem-Solving Skills: Strengthen the ability to analyse problems, identify potential solutions, and implement effective strategies. This skill set encourages a proactive approach to overcoming obstacles.

7. Reflect on Past Successes: Regular reflection on past instances of overcoming adversity can bolster self-efficacy and provide motivation for facing current challenges.

Resilience and Career Development: An Inextricable Link

The journey of career development, marked by its highs and lows, demands a resilience that is both enduring and adaptable. The setbacks encountered along this path—be they in the form of job loss, missed promotions, or failed projects—are not mere hindrances but integral components of the journey. They offer invaluable lessons, fostering a resilience that not only aids in recovery but also propels individuals towards greater levels of achievement and fulfillment.

In essence, the cultivation of resilience is a dynamic and continuous process, integral to navigating the complexities of modern careers. It is through embracing and overcoming adversity that individuals discover their true potential, refine their goals, and carve out paths that are not only successful but deeply rewarding. The psychology of resilience, therefore, is not merely an academic discourse but a practical blueprint for thriving in the ever-evolving landscape of professional development.

The Power of a Growth Mindset

In the evolving narrative of personal and professional development, the dichotomy of growth versus fixed mindsets, as illuminated by the pioneering work of Carol Dweck, offers profound insights into the nature of learning, resilience, and success. This conceptual framework not only categorises our intrinsic beliefs about learning and intelligence but also highlights the transformative potential of embracing a growth mindset. By exploring the characteristics of these mindsets and the impact of adopting a growth-oriented approach, we can uncover strategies for transforming challenges into springboards for learning and advancement.

At the heart of Dweck's theory is a simple yet revolutionary distinction: a fixed mindset assumes that our abilities, intelligence, and talents are static traits, leaving little room for growth or development. In contrast, a growth mindset thrives on challenge and sees failure not as evidence of unintelligence but as a heartening springboard for growth and for stretching our existing abilities. This shift in perspective is not merely academic; it is a powerful catalyst for change, influencing how individuals approach goals, confront challenges, and perceive their potential.

The Fixed Mindset: A Barrier to Progress

Individuals with a fixed mindset perceive their talents and intelligence as innate qualities that are immutable. This belief system can lead to a desire to appear smart or talented at all costs, often at the expense of genuine learning and growth. Challenges are avoided, effort is seen as fruitless if one is truly talented, and constructive criticism is ignored or even resented. The fixed mindset creates a psychological glass ceiling, limiting individuals' achievement and resilience in the face of adversity.

Embracing a Growth Mindset: A Path to Continuous Development

Conversely, the growth mindset is characterised by an underlying belief in the malleability of intelligence and abilities. Challenges are embraced, effort is viewed as the path to mastery, criticism is seen as a valuable source of feedback, and the success of others is an inspiration rather than a threat. This perspective fosters a relentless pursuit of self-improvement and a resilient approach to setbacks. The growth mindset, therefore, is not just about effort; it is about learning from every situation and persistently refining one's approach to achieve excellence.

Transforming Challenges into Opportunities

The shift from a fixed to a growth mindset can profoundly alter how individuals respond to challenges. Instead of viewing difficult tasks or setbacks as threats to their self-worth, those with a growth mindset see them as opportunities to expand their abilities and evolve. This shift is crucial in the professional realm, where innovation, continuous learning, and adaptability are prized.

Strategies for Cultivating a Growth Mindset

1. **Embrace Challenges:** Actively seek out new challenges as opportunities for learning and self-discovery. This approach will gradually build your confidence in handling difficult situations and reinforce your growth mindset.

2. **Persist in the Face of Setbacks:** View setbacks as part of the learning process rather than insurmountable obstacles. Analyse what went wrong, adjust your strategies, and try again with renewed determination.

3. **Value Effort:** Recognise that effort is a necessary component of success. Celebrate the hard work behind achievements, both yours and others', to reinforce the idea that perseverance is key to overcoming challenges.

4. **Learn from Criticism:** Instead of dismissing criticism, analyse it objectively, extract actionable insights, and apply this feedback to improve. This open-minded approach to feedback is a hallmark of the growth mindset.

5. **Be Inspired by the Success of Others:** Use the achievements of others as motivation to grow and learn. This not only cultivates a sense of possibility but also fosters a supportive and collaborative environment.

6. **Reflect on and Reassess Your Approach to Learning:** Regular self-reflection on your approach to learning and challenges can help identify areas where a fixed mindset may still be lingering. Commit to adjusting your perspective and strategies in these areas to foster a growth mindset.

The Impact of a Growth Mindset

Adopting a growth mindset can have a transformative impact on your professional life. It enables a more adventurous, resilient, and innovative approach to career development, encouraging continuous learning and adaptability in the face of change. The growth mindset liberates individuals from the fear of failure, opening up a world of possibilities for achievement and self-fulfilment.

In conclusion, the journey from a fixed to a growth mindset is both challenging and rewarding. It requires vigilance, persistence, and a commitment to personal development. Yet, the rewards—increased resilience, continuous learning, and greater success—are invaluable. By cultivating a growth mindset, we not only enhance our own career trajectories but also contribute to a culture of growth, innovation, and collective achievement. In the vast landscape of the mind, a growth mindset is the fertile ground from which the seeds of potential can sprout and flourish, transforming the way we approach our careers and our lives.

Cultivating Well-being

In the relentless pursuit of career success, the imperative of self-care often fades into the background, overshadowed by the demands of professional achievements and milestones. Yet, the nurturing of personal well-being is not merely a complementary aspect of a thriving career; it is its bedrock. This exploration delves into the critical role that self-care plays in facilitating professional growth, offering insights into maintaining a healthy work-life balance, managing stress effectively, and incorporating mindfulness practices into daily routines.

The Foundation of Professional Growth

The journey towards professional success is marred by challenges, obstacles, and pressures that test our resilience, adaptability, and endurance. In navigating these challenges, the role of self-care emerges as foundational, serving as a catalyst for sustained productivity, creativity, and motivation. Far from being a luxury or an afterthought, self-care is a strategic imperative that enhances our capacity to perform at our peak, overcome adversity, and achieve our career objectives.

Work-Life Balance: Striking the Right Chord

Achieving a healthy work-life balance is a critical aspect of self-care, ensuring that our pursuit of professional aspirations does not come at the expense of personal well-being, relationships, and leisure. This balance is not a one-size-fits-all formula but a personalised harmony that accommodates the unique demands of one's profession, personal life, and health. It involves setting clear boundaries between work and personal time, prioritising tasks effectively, and ensuring that time is allocated not just to professional duties but also to activities that rejuvenate the mind, body, and spirit.

Managing Stress: Navigating Professional Pressures

Stress is an inescapable companion on the path to career success, emanating from deadlines, performance expectations, and the challenges of navigating complex workplace dynamics. Effective stress management, therefore, becomes crucial in maintaining mental and emotional equilibrium. Techniques such as deep breathing exercises, regular physical activity, and engaging in hobbies or interests outside of work can serve as effective stress relievers. Additionally, developing a problem-solving mindset towards work-related challenges, rather than perceiving them as threats, can mitigate stress levels and foster a more productive and positive work environment.

Mindfulness Practices: Cultivating Presence and Focus

Incorporating mindfulness practices into one's daily routine can significantly enhance professional growth by improving focus, emotional regulation, and decision-making capacity. Mindfulness, the practice of being fully present and engaged in the moment without judgment, can be cultivated through meditation, mindful breathing, or even mindful walking. These practices help to clear the mind, reduce stress, and enhance concentration, thereby improving productivity and creativity at work. Moreover, mindfulness fosters a deeper sense of self-awareness, enabling individuals to recognise their strengths, areas for improvement, and the alignment of their career path with their values and purpose.

Practical Tips for Integrating Self-Care into Professional Life

1. **Schedule Regular Breaks**: Integrate short breaks into your workday to rest and recharge. Even a few minutes spent away from your desk can improve mental clarity and reduce fatigue.

2. **Set Realistic Goals**: Avoid setting overly ambitious goals that lead to undue stress. Instead, aim for achievable objectives that motivate and provide a sense of accomplishment.

3. **Cultivate Healthy Relationships**: Foster positive relationships with colleagues, mentors, and peers. A supportive network can provide encouragement, advice, and a sense of belonging.

4. **Prioritise Physical Health**: Maintain a regular exercise routine, eat a balanced diet, and ensure adequate sleep. Physical health is intrinsically linked to mental and emotional well-being.

5. **Practise Gratitude**: Take time to reflect on and appreciate the successes, no matter how small. Cultivating gratitude can enhance overall happiness and satisfaction with life and work.

Integrating self-care in professional life is not merely a strategy for personal well-being but a cornerstone of career excellence. By prioritising work-life balance, managing stress effectively, and embracing mindfulness, individuals can enhance their resilience, productivity, and creativity. Self-care empowers professionals to navigate the complexities of their career journeys with grace, ensuring that the pursuit of success is balanced with the nurturing of personal health and happiness. In this harmonious integration of personal well-being and professional aspirations lies the secret to a fulfilling, successful career.

The Power of Celebrating Progress and Perseverance

In the grand narrative of professional and personal development, the milestones of progress and the resilience of perseverance often become submerged under the pursuit of major achievements. Yet, the art of acknowledging and celebrating these moments—regardless of their scale—is fundamental not only to sustaining motivation but also to nurturing a culture of appreciation and growth. This exploration delves into the significance of recognising every step forward and the enduring strength of perseverance, highlighting how these practices can catalyse momentum and foster a profound sense of fulfillment in the face of challenges.

The Psychology of Recognition

At the heart of celebrating progress lies a deep psychological need for recognition and validation. The human psyche thrives on acknowledgement, which acts as a powerful motivator and reinforces our commitment to our goals. Each act of recognition, no matter how small, serves as an affirmation of our efforts, transforming our perception of the journey from a series of tasks into a pathway marked by growth and achievement. This shift in perspective is crucial; it enables us to view challenges not as insurmountable obstacles but as opportunities for further development and success.

Momentum Through Micro-Achievements

The journey toward any significant goal is paved with countless micro-achievements—small, seemingly inconsequential successes that cumulatively contribute to the larger objective. Recognising these micro-achievements is akin to collecting the pieces of a puzzle; individually, they may seem trivial, but together, they form a complete picture of progress and purpose. Celebrating these moments builds momentum, creating a continuous cycle of positive reinforcement that propels us forward. It transforms the daunting expanse of the journey into manageable segments, each marked by its own victory and learning experience.

Perseverance as a Virtue

Perseverance, the steadfast determination to continue despite difficulties, is the silent companion of progress. It is the fuel that powers the engine of achievement, especially when the path is fraught with setbacks and failures. Acknowledging the role of perseverance in overcoming these challenges is essential; it highlights the strength and resilience inherent in the journey and reinforces the value of persistence. Celebrating perseverance reminds us that while the destination is important, the endurance and tenacity demonstrated along the way are equally worthy of honour.

Strategies for Celebrating Progress and Perseverance

1. **Reflective Journaling**: Regularly document your journey, noting both the achievements and the challenges overcome. This practice not only serves as a record of progress but also as a tool for reflection, enabling you to appreciate the depth of your perseverance.

2. **Set Regular Review Milestones**: Implement periodic review sessions to evaluate progress and acknowledge the efforts made. These sessions can be opportunities to celebrate achievements, reassess goals, and recalibrate strategies in light of new learnings.

3. **Share Your Journey**: Sharing your progress and the challenges you've overcome with mentors, peers, or

through social media can amplify the sense of achievement and provide external validation. It also offers an opportunity to inspire and encourage others on their paths.

4. **Reward Yourself**: Establish a system of rewards for achieving certain milestones or for persisting through particularly challenging periods. These rewards, whether they be simple pleasures or significant treats, serve as tangible markers of acknowledgment and celebration.

5. **Cultivate a Culture of Recognition**: For those in leadership positions, fostering an environment that recognises and celebrates the achievements and perseverance of others can enhance motivation, productivity, and morale within teams and organisations.

The Transformative Power of Acknowledgement

The act of celebrating progress and perseverance has a transformative impact on our journey. It not only bolsters motivation and resilience but also enhances our overall well-being and satisfaction. Recognising our achievements and the effort required to attain them imbues our work with meaning and purpose, transforming the professional journey into a rich tapestry of experiences, learnings, and accomplishments.

Moreover, this practice of acknowledgment encourages a mindset of gratitude and positivity, which can significantly influence our approach to future challenges and goals. It cultivates an attitude of hope and determination, essential qualities for navigating the complexities of personal and professional growth.

In essence, celebrating progress and perseverance is an art—a skill that enriches the narrative of achievement with layers of meaning and joy. It is a testament to the human spirit's capacity to aspire, endure, and ultimately triumph. By embracing this art, we not only acknowledge the milestones and resilience that characterise our journey but also honour the profound journey of growth itself.

Chapter 5: Practical Steps for Career Manifestation

Embarking on the journey of career manifestation requires more than just clarity of vision and the will to succeed. It demands a systematic approach, grounded in actionable steps and strategies, to turn aspirations into reality. "Practical Steps for Career Manifestation" is designed as a guide to traverse this journey, providing you with a comprehensive toolkit to actively shape your professional destiny. This chapter delves into the fabric of career development, weaving together essential strategies for building a robust career blueprint, enhancing your personal brand, nurturing strategic relationships, and continuously evolving through learning and adaptability.

The path to manifesting your career aspirations is multifaceted, encompassing the development of a strong personal brand that aligns with your professional identity and values. It extends into the art of networking, where meaningful connections are cultivated, not just for the opportunities they might directly provide but also for the wisdom, support, and mentorship they offer. Furthermore, this journey is underpinned by an unwavering commitment to skill acquisition and the pursuit of lifelong learning—a recognition that the landscape of industry and opportunity is ever-changing, and so too must be our toolkit for navigating it.

Yet, beyond the practical strategies for external advancement lies the internal journey of developing resilience and adaptability—qualities that enable us to navigate the uncertainties of the career path with grace and confidence. This chapter, therefore, not only equips you with the external tools for career progression but also guides you in cultivating the inner resources necessary for sustained success.

Through leveraging mentorship and coaching, we explore the transformative power of guidance from those who have navigated their own paths to success. This mentorship, whether formal or informal, acts as a compass, providing direction, insight, and encouragement. Simultaneously, mastering adaptability and resilience prepares you to face inevitable challenges and setbacks with a mindset geared towards growth and opportunity.

As you engage with the practical steps outlined in this chapter, you are invited to view your career not as a fixed trajectory but as a dynamic journey of growth, learning, and manifestation. Each strategy, each piece of advice, is a stepping stone towards realizing your career aspirations, crafted to empower you to take control of your professional journey and manifest the career you envision.

Embark on this chapter with an open mind and a readiness to act. The journey of career manifestation is as much about the destination as it is about the path you forge to get there. Let this guide serve as your roadmap, illuminating the way forward with practical steps and insights designed to turn your career aspirations into tangible achievements.

The Essence of a Visionary Career Blueprint

In the grand narrative of professional growth, the creation of a visionary career blueprint stands as a pivotal chapter. This blueprint, far from being a rigid itinerary, is a living document that captures your aspirations, values, and purpose, guiding you through the intricacies of career development with intention and foresight. It is the art of translating abstract dreams into concrete plans, underpinned by a commitment to flexibility and adaptability. This exploration delves into the process of crafting such a blueprint, offering insights into envisioning your desired future, setting long-term goals, and delineating the steps necessary to manifest these aspirations.

Envisioning the Desired Future

The journey begins with a vision—a clear, compelling picture of the career you aspire to. This vision is not merely about job titles or accolades but about the impact you wish to make, the passions you desire to pursue, and the life you aim to lead. Envisioning your desired future requires introspection and imagination, asking yourself not only what success looks like but also what it feels like. Consider the roles, industries, and types of work that ignite your passion, the values you want your career to reflect, and the balance you seek between your professional and personal life. This vision forms the cornerstone of your career blueprint, providing direction and inspiration as you navigate your professional journey.

Setting Long-term Career Goals

With a vision in place, the next step is to translate this overarching dream into specific, long-term career goals. These goals should be ambitious yet attainable, serving as milestones on the path to your envisioned future. Setting effective goals involves a balance between aspiration and realism, ensuring that each goal is aligned with your values, leverages your strengths, and addresses areas for growth. It's important to articulate these goals with clarity, specifying the outcomes you aim to achieve, the timeframe for accomplishing them, and the criteria for measuring success.

Outlining the Steps to Achieve Your Goals

The essence of a career blueprint lies in its actionability—the detailed plans that outline how you will achieve your long-term goals. This involves breaking down each goal into smaller, manageable objectives and identifying the specific actions, resources, and timelines required to accomplish them. Consider the skills and knowledge you need to acquire, the relationships you need to build, and the experiences you need to gain. Plan for incremental progress, setting short-term objectives that cumulatively build towards your larger goals.

Emphasizing Flexibility and Adaptability

A visionary career blueprint, while detailed and structured, must also embrace flexibility and adaptability. The professional landscape is ever-evolving, marked by technological advancements, industry shifts, and unexpected opportunities. As such, your blueprint should be revisited and revised regularly, allowing you to pivot in response to new information, experiences, and changes in your personal and professional life. Flexibility in your plans enables you to seize unforeseen opportunities and navigate challenges without losing sight of your overarching vision and goals.

Strategies for Developing a Visionary Career Blueprint

1. **Reflect and Revise**: Dedicate time regularly to reflect on your career progress, revisiting your vision and goals to ensure they remain relevant and inspiring. Be open to

revising your blueprint as you grow and as the landscape around you changes.

2. **Seek Feedback and Guidance**: Engage with mentors, peers, and professionals in your field to gain insights and feedback on your career plans. Their perspectives can provide valuable validation and challenge your assumptions, fostering a more robust and realistic blueprint.

3. **Cultivate a Learning Mindset**: Adopt a mindset of continuous learning and curiosity, seeking out opportunities to expand your knowledge and skills. This commitment to personal and professional development is critical for adapting to change and achieving your career goals.

4. **Prioritize Self-awareness**: Keep self-awareness at the core of your career blueprint, regularly assessing your strengths, weaknesses, and passions. Understanding yourself deeply enables you to make decisions that align with your values and purpose.

Crafting a visionary career blueprint is an essential step in manifesting your professional aspirations. It provides a structured yet flexible framework for navigating the complexities of career development, rooted in a deep understanding of your values, strengths, and aspirations. By envisioning your desired future, setting long-term goals, and outlining actionable steps—while remaining open to adaptation and growth—you equip yourself with the tools to transform your career dreams into reality. This blueprint is not just a plan but a declaration of your commitment to leading a career marked by purpose, growth, and fulfillment.

The Art of Personal Branding in Professional Growth

In the contemporary professional arena, the concept of personal branding has transcended beyond a mere buzzword to become an essential strategy for career development and recognition. Personal branding, the deliberate and strategic effort to shape public perception of an individual, mirrors the essence of one's professional identity, values, and strengths. It's about curating the narrative of your professional life, ensuring that it accurately reflects who you are and the unique contributions you bring to your field. This exploration delves into the importance of building a strong personal brand and offers strategies for leveraging digital platforms and networking opportunities to showcase your expertise, connect with industry leaders, and enhance visibility in your chosen field.

The Foundation of a Strong Personal Brand

At its core, a strong personal brand is authentic, consistent, and visible. It's a reflection of your genuine self, your professional journey, and the values you uphold. Authenticity ensures that your brand resonates with truth and integrity, fostering trust and credibility. Consistency across all platforms and interactions reinforces your brand identity, making it easily recognizable. Visibility ensures that your brand reaches your intended audience, allowing your professional narrative to influence and inspire.

Authenticity: The Soul of Your Brand

The journey to building a personal brand begins with introspection. It's essential to identify and articulate what you stand for, your professional passions, and the unique skills and experiences that differentiate you from others. This authenticity becomes the soul of your brand, guiding the content you create, the messages you share, and the way you engage with your professional community.

Consistency: The Framework of Recognition

Consistency in your personal branding efforts helps in solidifying your professional image and ensures that your audience—be it potential employers, clients, or peers—receives a uniform message about who you are and what you offer. This includes consistent use of language, visuals, and themes across all your professional platforms, from your social media profiles to your personal website and offline networking.

Visibility: The Pathway to Influence

Enhancing the visibility of your personal brand requires strategic use of various platforms and tools. Here are several strategies to elevate your professional presence:

1. **Social Media Mastery**: Select social media platforms that align with your professional goals and audience. LinkedIn, for instance, is invaluable for professional networking and

thought leadership, while platforms like Twitter and Instagram can showcase your industry engagement and personal interests. Regularly posting insightful content, engaging with others' posts, and contributing to industry discussions can boost your visibility and position you as an expert in your field.

2. **Content Creation**: Blogging or producing content related to your field not only demonstrates your expertise but also adds value to your community. Whether it's through articles, videos, or podcasts, sharing your knowledge and perspectives can attract a following and open doors to new opportunities.

3. **Networking with Intent**: Build and nurture a network of professionals who share your interests or values. Attend industry events, participate in webinars, and engage in online forums. Networking isn't just about gaining visibility; it's about creating meaningful connections that can support and enrich your professional journey.

4. **Professional Platforms**: Beyond social media, platforms like Medium, GitHub (for developers), or Behance (for creatives) allow you to showcase your work and contribute to your field. Participation in these platforms can enhance your credibility and attract attention from industry leaders.

5. **Personal Website**: A personal website serves as the central hub for your personal brand, offering a comprehensive view of your professional journey, portfolio, and insights. It's a space entirely yours, allowing for full control over the narrative and presentation of your brand.

Navigating Challenges in Personal Branding

Building a personal brand is a dynamic and ongoing process, fraught with challenges such as maintaining authenticity in the face of changing trends or managing negative feedback. Overcoming these challenges involves staying true to your core values, being open to growth and learning, and engaging with your audience with transparency and integrity.

Embarking on the Branding Journey

The art of personal branding is not merely a self-promotion tactic but a strategic approach to professional growth and recognition. It's about intentionally crafting and communicating your professional narrative to align with your career aspirations, connecting with like-minded professionals, and making a meaningful impact in your field. By investing in the development of a strong, authentic, and visible personal brand, you equip yourself with a powerful tool to navigate the complexities of the professional world, paving the way for opportunities, influence, and success.

Mastering Strategic Networking and Relationship Building

In the intricate dance of professional advancement, the art of networking and relationship building emerges as a pivotal performance. Far from being mere social niceties, these practices are strategic tools that unlock doors to mentorship, collaborations, and opportunities, weaving the web of success in the vast expanse of one's career landscape. This exploration delves into practical methods for expanding professional networks and cultivating meaningful relationships within the industry, offering insights into effective networking practices both online and offline, and underscoring the importance of nurturing connections with intention and authenticity.

The Essence of Strategic Networking

Strategic networking transcends the act of collecting business cards or amassing LinkedIn connections; it's about establishing genuine connections that are mutually beneficial. The cornerstone of strategic networking is the recognition of its dual nature—it is both an art and a science, requiring a delicate balance of genuine interest in others and the strategic pursuit of professional growth.

Cultivating Meaningful Connections

The journey towards building a robust professional network begins with the cultivation of meaningful connections. This process involves engaging with individuals not merely as potential stepping stones but as partners in mutual growth. Meaningful connections are fostered through empathy, active listening, and a genuine interest in the professional journey of others. These relationships, rooted in trust and respect, are the bedrock upon which lasting professional networks are built.

Effective Networking Practices: Online and Offline

1. **Online Networking**: In the digital age, online platforms offer unprecedented opportunities for networking. LinkedIn, for instance, is a powerhouse for professional connections, allowing for the exploration of industries, companies, and potential mentors. Effective online networking involves engaging with content thoughtfully, sharing insights and knowledge, and reaching out with personalised messages that reflect a genuine interest in the other party's work and experiences. Joining industry-specific online forums and participating in webinars can also expand your network and visibility.

2. **Offline Networking**: Despite the digital revolution, offline networking retains its significance. Attending industry conferences, workshops, and seminars provides a platform for face-to-face interaction, forging connections that are often more impactful and memorable. When engaging in offline networking, the focus should be on quality over quantity—meaningful conversations with a few individuals can be more beneficial than superficial interactions with many.

Nurturing Connections for Mentorship and Opportunities

The true value of networking is realized in the nurturing of these connections. Regular follow-ups, sharing relevant information or articles, and offering assistance or support in their projects can strengthen relationships. Expressing appreciation for their advice or time, and keeping them informed about your progress, can also enhance the bond.

For those seeking mentorship, approaching potential mentors with specific requests for guidance, based on their expertise, increases the chances of a positive response. Demonstrating how their mentorship could shape your career can be a compelling reason for them to invest time in you.

Collaborations and Opportunities

Strategic networking also opens avenues for collaborations and opportunities. By engaging actively in professional communities and contributing to discussions, you can position yourself as a knowledgeable and collaborative individual. Collaborative projects, whether they are research, writing, or community initiatives, not only broaden your experience but also increase your visibility within your network.

Mastering the Balance

Effective networking and relationship building require mastering the balance between giving and taking. The principle of reciprocity plays a crucial role in the dynamics of professional relationships. Offering help, sharing knowledge, and being a reliable connection yourself encourages a culture of mutual support within your network.

Strategic networking and relationship building are critical components of professional success. They are not about opportunistic engagements but about fostering genuine connections that can support and enrich your career journey. By adopting effective networking practices, both online and offline, and nurturing these connections with care, you can build a network that not only supports your current professional needs but also adapts and grows with your career. In mastering these arts, you weave the web of success, creating a tapestry of relationships that supports, inspires, and propels you towards your professional aspirations.

Integrating Lifelong Learning into Your Career Strategy

In an era where the only constant is change, the ability to continually acquire new skills and embrace lifelong learning has become a cornerstone of professional resilience and growth. Gone are the days when education ended upon stepping out of the classroom. Today's rapidly evolving job market demands a proactive approach to skill acquisition and a commitment to ongoing personal development. This narrative is not just about staying relevant; it's about thriving, adapting, and discovering new horizons in one's career journey.

Recognizing the Importance of Continuous Learning

The landscape of work is being reshaped by technological advancements, shifts in economic structures, and evolving business models. In this dynamic environment, skill sets can become obsolete with alarming speed, and new opportunities often require a diverse and updated portfolio of abilities. Lifelong learning is the fuel that powers your career engine through these shifts, enabling you not just to keep pace but to steer your career with intention and vision.

Identifying Skill Gaps

The first step in the lifelong learning journey is the identification of skill gaps. This requires a keen self-awareness and an honest assessment of your current abilities against the backdrop of your career aspirations and the demands of the job market. Identifying these gaps is not an admission of inadequacy but a strategic move towards empowerment and growth. Regularly conducting a skills audit can help pinpoint areas for development, be it deepening expertise in your current field or branching out into new competencies.

Exploring Avenues for Education and Training

Once skill gaps are identified, the next step is to explore the myriad avenues available for education and training. The digital age has democratized access to learning, offering a plethora of options tailored to various needs, schedules, and learning styles:

1. **Online Courses**: Platforms such as Coursera, edX, and Udemy provide access to courses from leading universities and institutions around the world, covering a vast array of subjects and skills.

2. **Workshops and Seminars**: Often more interactive, workshops and seminars offer the opportunity to gain hands-on experience and can be found through professional associations, industry groups, or local educational institutions.

3. **Webinars and Podcasts**: For those who prefer learning on the go, webinars and podcasts can provide valuable insights and knowledge in a more digestible format.

4. **Certifications**: Pursuing professional certifications not only fills skill gaps but also adds a valuable credential to your resume, signaling your commitment to your profession.

Integrating Learning into Daily Routine

The challenge many face is not the lack of resources but finding the time to engage with these opportunities. Integrating learning into your daily routine requires intentionality and strategy. It could be as simple as dedicating a set time each day or week to learning, using breaks or commutes to listen to educational podcasts, or setting specific, achievable learning goals. The key is to view learning not as a task but as a natural and enjoyable part of your professional development.

Leveraging Learning for Career Advancement

The ultimate goal of continuous learning is to translate new knowledge and skills into career advancement. This involves not just acquiring skills in isolation but actively looking for ways to apply them in your current role, side projects, or within your professional community. Documenting your learning journey and achievements, updating your resume, and discussing your development in performance reviews can also highlight your initiative and commitment to growth.

Fostering a Culture of Learning

Beyond personal development, there's immense value in fostering a culture of learning within your professional network and organization. Sharing resources, initiating study groups, or even mentoring others can enrich the learning ecosystem, creating a mutually supportive environment that benefits everyone involved.

Embracing Adaptability

Lastly, embracing lifelong learning is about more than just acquiring new skills; it's about cultivating adaptability and a mindset open to change and growth. It's recognizing that every step in your learning journey is a step towards manifesting the career you envision, in an ever-changing professional landscape.

In summary, integrating lifelong learning into your career strategy is not just a means to an end but a fulfilling journey in its own right. It is a testament to the belief that growth, both personal and professional, is an unending quest—a quest that not only enhances your career prospects but enriches your life with knowledge, versatility, and the joy of continuous discovery.

Chapter 6: Navigating Career Transitions with Manifestation

Embarking on a career transition, whether seeking new job opportunities, aspiring for advancement, or contemplating a complete career change, is a journey filled with possibilities and challenges. It is a period that tests not only one's resilience and adaptability but also the clarity of one's professional aspirations. "Navigating Career Transitions with Manifestation" introduces a transformative approach to steering through these pivotal phases, by harmonizing practical career strategies with the profound principles of manifestation.

In this chapter, we explore how the power of manifestation—a process that involves setting clear intentions, embracing positive visualizations, and aligning actions with desired outcomes—can be leveraged to guide and enhance your career trajectory. This approach transcends traditional job search tactics, inviting you to delve deeper into the core of what you truly seek in your professional life and how you can actively attract these opportunities.

Through a series of carefully curated topics, we provide insights into developing a manifestation mindset tailored for job seekers, the importance of intention setting in achieving career growth, and the application of visualization techniques to foster successful transitions. We delve into the significance of affirmations and positive self-talk in overcoming the hurdles often encountered in the job search process and elucidate the concept of vibrational matching to attract the opportunities that resonate most deeply with your professional desires and values.

This chapter is designed to empower you with the knowledge and tools to not only navigate career transitions with confidence but also to craft a career path that is in profound alignment with your personal strengths, values, and aspirations. By integrating the principles of manifestation with actionable career strategies, you are invited to transform the way you approach job searches, career changes, or advancements—turning aspirations into tangible realities.

As you turn the pages, remember that career transitions are not merely steps towards new professional landscapes but are pivotal moments of growth and self-discovery. "Navigating Career Transitions with Manifestation" is your guide to embracing these transitions with intention, vision, and an unwavering belief in your ability to manifest the career of your dreams.

The Manifestation Mindset for Job Seekers

In the journey towards career fulfillment, job seekers often find themselves navigating a path fraught with uncertainty and competition. Amidst the challenges of job searching, the cultivation of a manifestation mindset emerges as a transformative strategy, not just to traverse this path but to attract opportunities that are in deep alignment with one's skills, values, and professional aspirations. This mindset, grounded in clarity, positivity, and visualization, serves as a beacon, guiding job seekers towards their desired career outcomes.

The Essence of Clarity in Career Manifestation

The first cornerstone of a manifestation mindset is clarity. Clarity about one's career goals acts as the compass in the vast sea of job opportunities, ensuring that every effort is directed towards destinations that resonate with one's professional identity and aspirations. Achieving this clarity involves deep introspection and honest assessment of one's skills, interests, and the impact one wishes to make through their work. It's about articulating not only the type of roles that appeal to you but also the environment, culture, and values of the organizations where you envision thriving.

Fostering Positivity Amidst Job Search Challenges

The job search journey is often marred by rejection and setbacks. Maintaining a positive outlook in the face of these challenges is crucial. Positivity in this context does not imply a naive optimism but a resilient mindset that chooses to focus on opportunities rather than obstacles. It's about embracing rejection as redirection—a sign that there are opportunities better suited to your skills and aspirations awaiting discovery. This positive outlook keeps motivation intact and fosters a proactive approach to job seeking, where each step, regardless of its immediate outcome, is viewed as progress.

The Power of Visualization

Visualization is a potent tool in the manifestation toolkit. It involves creating a vivid mental image of your desired career outcome, engaging all your senses to experience the achievement of your goal emotionally and psychologically before it materializes in the physical realm. This practice not only enhances motivation and focus but also subtly aligns your actions and decisions towards your goal. By regularly visualizing yourself succeeding in your desired role, negotiating your offer, or contributing to your ideal company, you prime your subconscious to identify and seize opportunities that can turn this vision into reality.

Aligning Actions with Aspirations

The manifestation mindset transcends mere thought and emotion; it necessitates action. This alignment of action with one's career aspirations is what propels the job seeker from dreaming to doing. It involves not only applying for jobs that fit your vision but also engaging in continuous learning to fill skill gaps, networking with professionals in your desired field, and personal branding that showcases your unique value proposition. Each action, informed by your clarity, positivity, and visualization, becomes a deliberate step towards manifesting your career goals.

Embracing Flexibility and Openness

While clarity and focus are vital, so too is the ability to remain flexible and open to unexpected opportunities. The job search process is dynamic, and opportunities that at first may not seem to align perfectly with your vision can sometimes offer new pathways to your goals. This openness, underpinned by a strong manifestation mindset, enables job seekers to explore a broader spectrum of possibilities, some of which may offer surprising avenues for professional growth and fulfillment.

Cultivating a Supportive Network

No journey of manifestation is complete without the support and guidance of others. Cultivating a network of mentors, peers, and professionals who share or support your vision can provide invaluable insights, encouragement, and opportunities. This supportive community not only enriches your job search experience but also amplifies your efforts to manifest your career goals, reminding you that you are not alone in this journey.

For job seekers navigating the complexities of the job market, adopting a manifestation mindset offers a strategic advantage. It empowers individuals to approach their job search with clarity, positivity, and purpose, transforming the process from a daunting challenge into a journey of opportunity and discovery. By cultivating this mindset, job seekers can attract opportunities that not only align with their skills and values but also contribute to their long-term professional growth and satisfaction. In essence, the manifestation mindset for job seekers is about envisioning success, engaging in actions that bring you closer to that vision, and remaining open to the myriad ways through which your career aspirations can materialize, crafting a fulfilling professional narrative that resonates with the essence of who you are and aspire to be.

The Transformative Power of Intention Setting in Career Advancements

In the realm of professional development, the act of setting intentions is akin to charting a course for a voyage across uncharted waters. It's about defining not just the destination but also the essence of the journey itself. Intention setting, when applied to career advancement, becomes a potent tool, guiding decision-making, networking, and personal branding efforts to unlock doors to new opportunities. This exploration delves into the art of setting powerful intentions for career growth, illuminating how these deliberate aims can shape your professional trajectory.

The Essence of Setting Intentions

At its core, setting intentions involves articulating clear and focused aims that reflect your desired outcomes in your career. Unlike goal-setting, which often focuses on measurable achievements, intention setting delves deeper into the why and how—the values, qualities, and attitudes you wish to bring to your professional endeavors. It's about establishing a mindset and an approach that will permeate every action and decision, thereby manifesting the career growth you seek.

Crafting Powerful Intentions

The process of crafting powerful intentions begins with reflection and clarity. It requires an honest assessment of your current professional state, your aspirations, and the gaps between the two. Powerful intentions are those that resonate deeply with your personal and professional values, are charged with positive energy, and are expressed in the present tense to create a sense of immediacy and reality.

For instance, instead of setting an intention like, "I want to be promoted," frame it as, "I bring leadership, creativity, and commitment to my team, contributing to our success and my career advancement." This not only defines the outcome but also encapsulates the qualities you intend to exhibit and the value you aim to add.

Intention Setting and Decision-Making

Intention setting becomes a compass for decision-making, enabling you to navigate career choices with confidence and purpose. When faced with decisions, large or small, refer back to your intentions. Ask yourself whether each choice aligns with the intentions you've set and whether it will propel you toward the professional growth you desire. This practice ensures that your career path is not shaped by chance or external pressures but by a deliberate pursuit of your envisioned future.

Networking with Intention

In the sphere of networking, intentions play a crucial role in shaping meaningful connections. Approach networking with the intention to build relationships based on mutual respect and shared values, rather than viewing contacts merely as stepping stones to your next opportunity. This shift in perspective fosters authentic interactions, making your networking efforts more fulfilling and likely to open doors to opportunities that align with your career aspirations.

Intention-Driven Personal Branding

Personal branding, too, benefits from the clarity and direction provided by intention setting. Define the core message and image you wish to convey in your professional sphere, ensuring it aligns with your career intentions. Every aspect of your personal brand, from your online presence to how you communicate in professional settings, should reflect these intentions. This coherence in your personal branding efforts enhances your visibility and positions you as a compelling candidate for advancement opportunities.

The Impact of Intention on Career Advancements

The impact of setting powerful intentions on career advancements is profound. Intentions act as the underlying current that propels your professional journey forward. They influence not just what you do but how you do it, imbuing your efforts with purpose and passion. As you align your actions with your intentions, you'll find that opportunities for growth and advancement begin to align with your path, drawn by the clarity and conviction with which you pursue your career objectives.

Moreover, intention setting fosters a proactive mindset, encouraging you to seek out opportunities, take on challenges, and continuously evolve in your professional capacity. It transforms the pursuit of career advancements from a reactive endeavor into a creative and dynamic process.

Embracing the Journey with Intention

Setting intentions for career advancement is not a one-time act but an ongoing practice that accompanies you throughout your professional journey. It requires regular reflection, adjustment, and reaffirmation as your career evolves and as new opportunities and challenges arise.

In essence, the art of intention setting in career advancements is about more than achieving specific milestones. It's about shaping a career that is not only successful by external measures but also deeply fulfilling and aligned with your core values and aspirations. By charting your course with intention, you unlock the transformative power to navigate your professional voyage with confidence, purpose, and a sense of boundless possibility.

Mastering Visualization Techniques for Career Transitions

In the tapestry of professional development, the act of transitioning—be it changing roles, industries, or embarking on advancement within one's current path—presents both a challenge and an opportunity. Navigating these waters with success often requires more than just a well-crafted resume or a robust network; it calls for a profound internal alignment of one's aspirations and energies. This is where the power of visualization, a technique rooted in the principles of manifestation, becomes a critical tool. By envisioning success in career transitions, individuals can align their subconscious with their conscious goals, thereby attracting the outcomes they desire. This exploration delves into the art of using visualization techniques throughout the stages of career transition, including preparation for job interviews, networking events, and crucial meetings that could pave the way for advancement.

The Foundation of Effective Visualization

Visualization is the process of creating a vivid and detailed mental image of a desired outcome, engaging all the senses to deepen the experience. The effectiveness of visualization lies in its ability to make aspirations feel attainable, thereby boosting confidence and motivation. To harness this power, one must begin with clarity—defining with precision the outcomes they seek from their career transition, whether it's securing a particular role, succeeding in a new industry, or achieving a significant career milestone.

Before the Transition: Setting the Stage

The journey of a successful career transition begins long before the actual move. During this preparatory phase, visualization techniques can be used to set the stage for success:

1. **Crafting Your Vision**: Dedicate time to meditate on your career aspirations, visualizing not only the ultimate goal but also the steps and milestones along the way. Imagine yourself mastering new skills, connecting with influential figures in your field, and contributing value in your new role.

2. **Creating a Vision Board**: Translate your mental visualizations into a physical or digital vision board. Include images, quotes, and symbols that represent your career goals and the transition you wish to make. This board will serve as a constant reminder and source of inspiration on your journey.

During the Transition: Amplifying Your Intentions

As you actively engage in job searches, prepare for interviews, or attend networking events, visualization can amplify your intentions and enhance your presence:

1. **Visualizing Success in Interviews and Meetings**: Before interviews or important meetings, take a few moments to visualize a positive outcome. Imagine yourself answering questions with confidence, connecting genuinely with your interviewers, and leaving a lasting impression. Envision the affirmative feedback and the eventual offer letter, feeling the emotions associated with these successes.

2. **Energizing Networking Efforts**: Prior to attending networking events, visualize yourself forming meaningful connections, engaging in enriching conversations, and leaving with new contacts who are eager to support your career transition. See these connections leading to valuable opportunities and insights.

After the Transition: Solidifying Your Place

Even after a successful career move, visualization remains a potent tool for ensuring long-term success and satisfaction:

1. **Visualizing Growth and Contributions**: Regularly visualize yourself excelling in your new role, growing professionally, and making significant contributions. Envision the positive impacts of your work on your team, organization, and industry.

2. **Projecting Future Successes**: Continue to use visualization to project future career milestones within your new path. Whether it's leading a high-stakes project, earning a promotion, or being recognized for your contributions, these visualizations can guide your ongoing efforts and development.

Integrating Visualization into Daily Routine

For visualization to be most effective, it should be integrated into your daily routine. This can be through dedicated meditation sessions, the use of affirmations that reinforce your visualized outcomes, or the practice of mindful reflection on your vision board.

The key is consistency and emotional engagement, allowing the power of visualization to align your subconscious mind with your conscious career aspirations.

The journey of career transition, marked by uncertainty and opportunity, requires not just strategic planning but also a deep internal alignment with one's goals. Visualization techniques offer a powerful means to achieve this alignment, turning the abstract into the attainable and the dreams into reality. By mastering these techniques, professionals can navigate the waters of career transition with confidence, clarity, and a heightened sense of purpose, making each step an intentional stride towards the manifestation of their career aspirations.

The Role of Affirmations in Navigating Career Transitions

Embarking on a job search or facing a career transition can often feel like navigating a maze fraught with uncertainty, rejections, and obstacles. In these moments, the resilience of the human spirit is tested, and the power of one's inner dialogue comes to the fore. Affirmations and positive self-talk emerge not merely as psychological panaceas but as essential tools for maintaining motivation, fostering resilience, and transforming challenges into stepping stones towards success. This exploration delves into the transformative potential of affirmations and positive self-talk, illuminating how they can be harnessed to navigate the intricacies of job searches and career changes with grace and determination.

The Power of Positive Self-Talk

At the heart of every job search challenge lies an opportunity for growth, provided we are prepared to listen, learn, and adapt. The narratives we tell ourselves in moments of doubt and rejection shape our reality and our responses to it. Positive self-talk is about consciously choosing words that affirm our capabilities, worth, and potential, counteracting the negative chatter that can all too easily derail our efforts. It is the practice of being your own coach, mentor, and cheerleader, reminding yourself of your strengths, resilience, and the value you bring to potential employers.

Crafting Effective Affirmations

Affirmations are positive, empowering statements that, when repeated with conviction and regularity, have the power to reprogram the subconscious mind, influence behaviour, and manifest desired outcomes. Effective affirmations are present-tense, positive, personal, and precise. For instance, affirming "I am a skilled and passionate professional, attracting opportunities that align with my strengths and values" reinforces a sense of self-worth and purpose, turning the job search into a journey of meaningful opportunities rather than a slog through rejection.

Integrating Affirmations into the Job Search Process

1. **Starting the Day with Purpose**: Begin each day of your job search or career transition with a set of personalized affirmations. Repeat them aloud or write them down in a journal. This practice sets a positive tone for the day, focusing your energy on possibilities and your capacity to seize them.

2. **Reframing Rejection**: After a setback or rejection, utilize affirmations to reframe the experience. Remind yourself that every "no" is a step closer to the "yes" that matters. An affirmation like "I am resilient, learning from each experience and moving closer to my ideal job" can shift the focus from failure to learning and growth.

3. **Preparing for Interviews**: Prior to interviews or important networking events, use affirmations to bolster your confidence and calm nerves. Affirmations such as "I communicate with clarity and confidence, making a positive impression" can prime you for success, enhancing your performance.

The Science Behind Affirmations

The efficacy of affirmations and positive self-talk is grounded in neuroplasticity—the brain's ability to reorganize itself by forming new neural connections throughout life. Regularly engaging in positive self-talk and affirmations can reshape our thought patterns, leading to increased self-esteem, better stress management, and a more optimistic outlook on the job search process. This mental shift not only improves our emotional and psychological well-being but also enhances our engagement with the job search process, making us more likely to identify and pursue opportunities.

Cultivating a Mindset of Resilience

Resilience is not inherent but cultivated through practices that fortify the spirit and mind. In the context of job searches and career changes, resilience is about more than enduring; it's about thriving amidst uncertainty. Affirmations and positive self-talk are integral to this process, helping to maintain focus on goals, persevere through challenges, and remain open to learning and adaptation.

Navigating the challenges of job searches and career transitions requires more than qualifications and experience; it demands a mindset geared towards growth, resilience, and positivity. Affirmations and positive self-talk are powerful allies in this journey, enabling individuals to maintain motivation, overcome obstacles, and manifest the career success they seek. By harnessing the transformative power of inner dialogue, job seekers and career changers can navigate the complexities of their professional paths with confidence, purpose, and an unwavering belief in their potential to achieve greatness.

The Art of Vibrational Matching in Career Advancement

In the quest for professional fulfillment, the principle of vibrational matching emerges as a profound yet often overlooked strategy. Rooted in the law of attraction, this concept suggests that by aligning one's vibrational energy with that of desired outcomes, individuals can attract opportunities, people, and circumstances that resonate with their aspirations. This exploration delves into the essence of vibrational matching within the context of career manifestation, guiding readers on harmonizing their energies and actions with the frequencies of the opportunities they seek.

Understanding Vibrational Matching

At its core, vibrational matching is about energetic alignment. Everything in the universe, including our thoughts, feelings, and desires, operates at a specific vibrational frequency. When we align our internal vibration with that of our desired career outcomes, we create a magnetic pull, attracting those very opportunities towards us. This alignment is not merely about wishful thinking but involves a deliberate calibration of our thoughts, emotions, and actions towards our professional goals.

Cultivating a High Vibrational State

Achieving vibrational matching begins with cultivating a high vibrational state—a state characterized by positive emotions, thoughts, and a deep sense of purpose. This state enhances your energetic presence, making you more attractive to opportunities that match your professional aspirations. Practices such as gratitude, meditation, and engaging in activities that bring joy and fulfillment can elevate your vibrational frequency, setting the foundation for vibrational matching.

Aligning Thoughts and Emotions with Career Aspirations

The thoughts we harbor and the emotions we nurture play a pivotal role in vibrational matching. To attract career opportunities that align with your goals, it's crucial to maintain a focus on positive, empowering thoughts and to cultivate emotions such as enthusiasm, confidence, and passion. Visualizing your career success, embracing the feeling of achievement, and maintaining an optimistic outlook, even in the face of challenges, are essential practices. This alignment ensures that your internal state resonates with the success you seek, drawing it into your experience.

Action as a Conduit for Vibrational Matching

While aligning your vibrational energy is fundamental, vibrational matching also demands action. Actions that are in harmony with your career goals serve as powerful signals to the universe, amplifying your intentions and attracting opportunities. Whether it's pursuing further education, networking within your desired industry, or taking on projects that showcase your skills and passion, each action should be imbued with intention and aligned with the vibrational frequency of your aspirations.

Navigating Rejections and Setbacks

The journey towards career manifestation is often met with rejections and setbacks. Within the framework of vibrational matching, these experiences are not seen as failures but as feedback mechanisms. They offer insights into areas of misalignment and opportunities to refine your vibrational frequency. Embracing a perspective of learning and growth allows you to maintain a high vibrational state, even in the face of adversity, ensuring that you remain in alignment with your desired outcomes.

The Role of Patience and Trust

Vibrational matching requires patience and trust in the timing and wisdom of the universe. The manifestation of career opportunities may not always follow a linear or predictable path. Cultivating patience and maintaining trust in the process are vital, as they keep your vibrational energy aligned with your goals, even when the outcomes are not immediately visible. Trust that every action taken in alignment will eventually lead you to the opportunities best suited for your growth and fulfillment.

Vibrational matching in the context of career advancement is an art that blends the energetic with the practical. It invites individuals to harmonize their internal states with the external manifestations they seek, creating a powerful attraction force for opportunities that resonate with their professional aspirations. By cultivating a high vibrational state, aligning thoughts and emotions with career goals, taking intentional action, and navigating challenges with resilience, individuals can navigate the journey of career manifestation with grace and efficacy. Embracing vibrational matching is to step into a realm of possibility, where the alignment of energy and action opens doors to opportunities that reflect one's highest aspirations and potential.

Chapter 7: Maintaining Alignment and Purpose Over Time

In the evolving journey of professional growth, maintaining alignment with one's career path and personal purpose presents a unique challenge. As we navigate through different stages of life and career, our aspirations, values, and circumstances invariably transform. This dynamic interplay between personal evolution and professional development requires not just adaptability but a conscious effort to sustain alignment and purpose over time. "Maintaining Alignment and Purpose Over Time" delves into the art and science of ensuring that your career trajectory remains congruent with your evolving self and the shifting landscapes of the professional world.

This chapter unfolds the strategies and practices essential for this sustained alignment, recognizing that the journey is as much about internal recalibration as it is about external adaptation. From the nuanced process of continually reassessing and realigning career paths with changing personal purposes to the application of long-term manifestation techniques, this chapter offers a blueprint for navigating the complexities of career and life transitions.

We explore the critical competencies of resilience and flexibility, which empower individuals to embrace change not as a barrier but as a catalyst for growth and renewal. Additionally, we delve into the integration of work-life harmony practices, emphasizing the importance of balance as a cornerstone of maintaining alignment with one's career and personal aspirations over the long haul.

The role of continuous learning and skill development is also examined, highlighting the necessity of perpetual growth and adaptation in response to the ever-evolving demands of the job market and one's own aspirations. This chapter provides not just a framework but also practical tools and insights for anyone looking to navigate their career with intention, purpose, and adaptability.

As we venture through "Maintaining Alignment and Purpose Over Time," we invite you to engage deeply with the concepts and strategies presented, viewing them as companions on your journey of professional development. This chapter is designed to serve as a guide for those committed to fostering a career that not only achieves success by external standards but also resonates deeply with their evolving personal narrative and purpose.

Realigning Career Paths with Personal Evolution

In the intricate dance of professional life, the alignment between career paths and personal purposes is not a one-time act but an ongoing process of adaptation and reflection. As individuals grow and evolve, so too do their aspirations, values, and definitions of success. This dynamic harmony requires a deliberate approach to continually reassess and realign career objectives with personal growth, ensuring that one's professional journey remains not only relevant but deeply fulfilling. This exploration delves into the importance of periodic self-reflection in career planning, alongside the tools and practical steps necessary for effective reassessment and realignment of career paths.

The Imperative of Periodic Self-Reflection

The cornerstone of sustained alignment in one's career is the practice of periodic self-reflection and evaluation. In a world that is constantly changing, where new opportunities and challenges emerge with increasing velocity, pausing to reflect on one's career trajectory and its congruence with evolving personal purposes is essential. This reflective practice serves as a compass, guiding individuals through the complexities of professional development and ensuring that their career path resonates with their current aspirations and values. It is through this introspection that one can discern shifts in personal goals and identify the need to pivot or adjust career strategies accordingly.

Tools and Techniques for Effective Reassessment

Embarking on the journey of career reassessment necessitates a structured approach, employing tools and techniques that facilitate a comprehensive evaluation of one's professional life in relation to personal growth.

1. **Career Audits**: Conducting a career audit involves a thorough examination of one's professional experiences,

achievements, and setbacks. This process enables individuals to assess the progress made towards their career objectives, the skills and knowledge acquired, and the alignment of their career trajectory with their evolving personal purposes.

2. **Personal SWOT Analyses**: Borrowed from the realms of business strategy, a personal SWOT analysis (Strengths, Weaknesses, Opportunities, Threats) offers a framework for assessing one's professional standing. By identifying strengths to capitalize on, weaknesses to address, opportunities to seize, and potential threats to mitigate, individuals can craft a nuanced strategy for career development that aligns with their personal evolution.

Practical Steps for Realigning Career Objectives

The process of realigning career paths with updated personal goals and purposes involves several practical steps, each designed to bridge the gap between where one stands and where one aspires to be.

1. **Defining Evolving Goals and Values**: The first step in realignment is the clear articulation of your evolved goals, values, and definitions of success. This may involve envisioning the desired state of your professional and personal life, identifying the values that are most important to you now, and setting new goals that reflect these priorities.

2. **Gap Analysis**: With a clear understanding of your updated goals and purposes, conduct a gap analysis to identify the discrepancies between your current career state and your desired future. This analysis should cover skill gaps, knowledge deficiencies, and any misalignments in your current role or industry.

3. **Strategic Action Planning**: Armed with insights from your gap analysis, develop a strategic action plan that outlines the steps needed to realign your career. This may involve pursuing further education or training, seeking new roles or projects that are more closely aligned with your evolved purposes, or even changing industries.

4. **Seeking Feedback and Mentorship**: Engage with mentors, peers, and professionals within your desired field to gain insights, feedback, and guidance on your realignment plan. Their perspectives can offer invaluable advice on navigating your career transition effectively.

5. **Implementing and Monitoring Progress**: With a strategic action plan in hand, implement the necessary changes and regularly monitor your progress. This should include revisiting your goals and plans periodically to ensure they remain aligned with your personal evolution.

Embracing Flexibility and Adaptability

The journey of realigning career paths with personal purposes underscores the importance of flexibility and adaptability. As individuals grow and their life circumstances change, so too might their professional aspirations and needs. Embracing this fluidity, and viewing career development as a dynamic and iterative process, allows individuals to navigate their professional lives with agility, ensuring that their career paths not only lead to success but to personal fulfillment and purpose.

In essence, the dynamic harmony between career paths and personal evolution is achieved through deliberate reflection, structured reassessment, and strategic action. By continually aligning one's professional journey with evolving personal purposes, individuals can craft a career that is not only successful but deeply resonant with the core of who they are and aspire to become.

Embracing Long-term Manifestation for Life and Career Evolution

In the journey of life and career, change is the only constant. As we navigate through various stages, from the zeal of early career days to the reflective periods of mid-career shifts and beyond, the ability to adapt and manifest desired outcomes becomes invaluable. Long-term manifestation techniques offer a compass by which to steer through these changes, not merely to weather the transitions but to thrive within them. This exploration delves into the art of long-term manifestation, a practice that harmonizes the power of intention with the fluidity of life's and career's evolving stages.

The Foundation of Long-term Manifestation

At its core, long-term manifestation is about setting intentions that transcend immediate goals and encompass broader visions for one's life and career. It involves a deep connection with one's inner self and a clear understanding of one's values, desires, and purposes that endure through life's transitions. This foundational clarity acts as the bedrock upon which the edifice of one's future is built, guiding choices, actions, and reactions through the myriad paths life may take.

Cultivating a Vision that Grows with You

The first step in long-term manifestation is to cultivate a vision that is both expansive and adaptable. This vision, while anchored in core values and long-term aspirations, allows room for growth, learning, and change. It is not a rigid endpoint but a living, breathing aspiration that evolves as you do. Envisioning your future in this way involves regular reflection and revisitation of your goals and desires, ensuring they remain aligned with your growing self and changing circumstances.

Practical Techniques for Long-term Manifestation

1. **Vision Boards and Journals**: Creating a vision board or journal that reflects your long-term aspirations can serve as a powerful visual and narrative reminder of your goals. These tools should be dynamic, updated regularly to reflect your evolving vision and to incorporate insights gained from experiences and reflections.

2. **Affirmations and Visualization**: Affirmations are positive statements that reinforce your ability to manifest your desired future, while visualization involves mentally picturing this future with as much detail and emotion as possible. Practicing these techniques regularly helps to align your subconscious with your long-term aspirations, embedding your vision deeply within your psyche.

3. **Milestone Mapping**: Breaking down your long-term vision into milestones and associated actions can make the journey more manageable and concrete. This approach allows you to celebrate progress, reassess direction, and

adjust plans as necessary, ensuring that your actions remain aligned with your evolving aspirations.

4. **Mindful Adaptability**: Cultivating an attitude of mindful adaptability involves being present with the current realities of your career and life while maintaining a connection to your long-term vision. It means being open to detours and unexpected opportunities, viewing them as potential pathways rather than distractions from your goals.

5. **Energy Alignment**: Long-term manifestation also involves aligning your energy—your emotions, thoughts, and actions—with your goals. This alignment is about embodying the qualities and energies of the future you wish to create, thereby attracting experiences, people, and opportunities that resonate with your vision.

Navigating Transitions with Grace

Life's transitions, whether expected or unforeseen, can often feel like upheavals, challenging our sense of stability and direction. Long-term manifestation techniques provide a framework for navigating these periods with grace. They remind us to return to our core values and vision, use changes as opportunities for growth, and realign our strategies and actions with our long-term aspirations.

The Role of Community and Mentorship

No journey of manifestation is solitary. Building a community of like-minded individuals and seeking mentorship can provide support, inspiration, and practical advice as you navigate your path. Sharing your vision and learning from the experiences of others can reinforce your commitment to your goals and provide new perspectives on achieving them.

Embracing the Journey

Ultimately, long-term manifestation is about embracing the journey of life and career with openness, intention, and purpose. It acknowledges that while we may set the direction, the paths we take are rich with learning and growth. By employing manifestation techniques tailored for the long haul, we equip ourselves with the tools to adapt to change, overcome obstacles, and realize our evolving aspirations.

In essence, long-term manifestation is a commitment to oneself—a commitment to grow, evolve, and thrive through the stages of life and career. It is about setting a course guided by deep-seated values and aspirations, being open to life's infinite possibilities, and actively shaping the future we desire. This approach not only enhances our ability to navigate the flux of life and career but also enriches our journey with purpose, fulfillment, and joy.

Fostering Resilience and Flexibility in Your Career Journey

In the ever-evolving tapestry of the professional world, change is not just a possibility; it's a guarantee. Whether it's technological advancements, shifts in market demands, or personal life changes, navigating through these transitions requires more than just technical expertise or experience. At the heart of a sustainable career, journey lies the twin pillars of resilience and flexibility. These core competencies are indispensable in maintaining alignment with one's career path and purpose over time. This exploration delves into the importance of cultivating a resilient mindset and the ability to adapt one's career trajectory, viewing change not as a hurdle but as a catalyst for growth and transformation.

The Bedrock of Resilience

Resilience is the psychological fortitude that enables individuals to bounce back from setbacks, challenges, and failures. It's about facing adversity head-on, learning from it, and emerging stronger. In the context of a career, resilience is what allows professionals to navigate through rejections, job losses, or unanticipated shifts in their field with grace and determination. Developing a resilient mindset begins with embracing a perspective that views challenges as opportunities for learning and growth. It involves:

1. **Practicing Optimism**: Cultivating an optimistic outlook enables you to see beyond temporary setbacks and focus on long-term goals. It's about trusting in your abilities to overcome obstacles and viewing each challenge as a stepping stone towards your aspirations.

2. **Building Emotional Intelligence**: Emotional intelligence, the ability to understand and manage your emotions and

those of others, is key to resilience. It allows for better stress management, enhances empathy, and facilitates constructive responses to feedback and criticism.

3. **Establishing a Support Network**: A robust support network of colleagues, mentors, and peers can provide encouragement, advice, and a fresh perspective, reinforcing your resilience in the face of career challenges.

The Virtue of Flexibility

Flexibility in one's career involves the willingness and capacity to adapt to changing circumstances, pivot strategies, and explore new opportunities. It's about letting go of rigid expectations and remaining open to uncharted paths that may lead to fulfilling outcomes. Cultivating flexibility requires:

1. **Continuous Learning**: Staying abreast of industry trends, emerging technologies, and new skill sets keeps you versatile and prepared to seize diverse opportunities.

2. **Embracing Uncertainty**: Developing comfort with uncertainty and ambiguity allows you to make decisions and take calculated risks, even when the outcome isn't guaranteed.

3. **Adaptive Planning**: Setting goals that are specific yet adaptable enables you to adjust your plans as new information and opportunities arise, ensuring your career path remains aligned with your evolving personal and professional landscape.

Strategies for Cultivating Resilience and Flexibility

Integrating resilience and flexibility into your career development involves a conscious and deliberate approach. Some strategies include:

- **Reflective Practice**: Regular reflection on your experiences, challenges faced, and lessons learned can deepen your resilience and enhance your adaptability.

- **Mindfulness and Stress Management**: Practices such as mindfulness meditation can improve emotional regulation, reduce stress, and enhance clarity of thought, contributing to both resilience and flexibility.

- **Scenario Planning**: Anticipating potential career scenarios and formulating response strategies can prepare you for change, making transitions smoother and less daunting.

- **Seeking Diverse Experiences**: Actively seeking out diverse professional experiences, such as cross-functional projects, industry conferences, or volunteer work, can broaden your perspectives, making you more adaptable to change.

The journey through the professional landscape is marked by continuous change and evolution. Cultivating resilience and flexibility is not merely about survival but about thriving in this dynamic environment. By developing a resilient mindset that embraces change as an opportunity for growth and fostering the flexibility to adapt one's career trajectory, professionals can navigate through transitions with confidence and purpose. These competencies ensure that, no matter how the external world shifts, one remains steadfastly aligned with their career path and purpose, ready to transform every gust of change into a wind that propels them forward on their career journey.

The Art of Work-Life Balance in Career Fulfillment

In the relentless pursuit of professional excellence, the delicate equilibrium between career aspirations and personal well-being often finds itself threatened. The quest for career success, while noble, can inadvertently overshadow the equally significant realms of personal health, relationships, and inner peace. It is here that the concept of work-life harmony emerges as a guiding principle, advocating not for a rigid division between professional and personal life, but for a fluid integration that honors and sustains both. This exploration delves into practical approaches to achieving and maintaining work-life harmony, emphasizing the critical role it plays in nurturing long-term alignment with both career and personal goals.

The Philosophy of Work-Life Harmony

At its essence, work-life harmony is the practice of blending one's professional and personal life in a way that enriches both domains.

Unlike the concept of work-life balance, which often implies a strict segregation of work and personal activities, work-life harmony acknowledges the interconnectedness of these aspects of life. It seeks to create a synergy where each facet supports and enhances the other, leading to a more fulfilling and sustainable lifestyle.

Setting Boundaries for Work and Life

The foundation of work-life harmony lies in the ability to set clear and firm boundaries. This involves delineating the time and space dedicated to work and ensuring it does not encroach upon personal time reserved for self-care, family, and leisure. It may require practical measures such as turning off work notifications outside of business hours, creating a dedicated workspace separate from personal spaces, or establishing clear communication with colleagues and employers about your availability.

Prioritizing Self-Care and Personal Well-being

Central to the pursuit of work-life harmony is the prioritization of self-care and personal well-being. This encompasses a wide array of practices, from ensuring adequate rest and nutrition to engaging in regular physical activity and mindfulness practices. Self-care acts as a counterbalance to work-related stress, replenishing one's energy reserves and ensuring that career pursuits do not come at the expense of health and vitality.

Implementing Practices for Harmonious Integration

Achieving work-life harmony requires intentional practices that facilitate the seamless integration of career and personal life. Some strategies include:

- **Effective Time Management**: Utilizing tools and techniques to manage time efficiently can help ensure that both work and personal activities receive the attention they deserve. This may involve task prioritization, delegation, and the use of productivity apps to streamline work processes.

- **Mindful Technology Use**: Being mindful of technology use, particularly social media and work-related communication outside office hours, can prevent work from dominating personal time. Establishing tech-free zones or times can help foster real connections with family and friends.

- **Regular Check-ins with Self**: Periodically checking in with oneself to assess levels of satisfaction and fulfillment in both work and personal life can provide insights into areas that may need adjustment. This reflective practice allows for continual realignment with one's values and goals.

- **Nurturing Relationships**: Actively nurturing relationships with family, friends, and community provides a support network that enriches personal life and can offer perspective and support through work-related challenges.

The Role of Employers in Supporting Work-Life Harmony

While much of the responsibility for achieving work-life harmony lies with the individual, employers also play a crucial role. Organizations that recognize the importance of their employees' well-being and work-life harmony are more likely to see enhanced productivity, lower turnover rates, and higher employee satisfaction. Practices such as flexible working hours, the provision of wellness programs, and encouraging time off can contribute significantly to an environment that supports work-life harmony.

Conclusion

The journey towards work-life harmony is both a personal and professional endeavor, requiring mindfulness, discipline, and a commitment to one's overall well-being. By integrating practical approaches to set boundaries, prioritize self-care, and implement harmonizing practices, individuals can navigate their careers with fulfillment and resilience. This harmonious integration ensures that career advancements and personal life not only coexist but thrive together, leading to a richer, more balanced life. As we navigate our paths, let us remember that the true measure of success is not just in the heights we reach in our careers but in the harmony we cultivate in our lives.

Embracing Continuous Learning in Your Career Journey

In an era defined by rapid technological advancements and shifting economic landscapes, the concept of a linear, unchanging career path has become antiquated. Today's professionals face a dynamic environment where the only constant is change itself. Within this context, continuous learning and skill development emerge not just as beneficial but essential practices for those seeking to maintain relevance and thrive professionally. This exploration delves into the significance of lifelong learning, highlighting its pivotal role in aligning one's career trajectory with evolving industry trends and personal aspirations.

The Imperative of Lifelong Learning

The journey of continuous learning begins with an acknowledgment of the ever-evolving nature of knowledge and industry demands. As new technologies emerge and old ones become obsolete, the skills that once guaranteed success can quickly lead to stagnation if not updated. Moreover, the pursuit of personal growth and fulfillment increasingly requires adaptability and a willingness to acquire new competencies. In this landscape, lifelong learning stands as a beacon, guiding individuals towards sustained employability and personal actualization.

Identifying Emerging Skill Requirements

Staying ahead in one's career necessitates a proactive approach to identifying emerging skills and knowledge areas. This process involves:

- **Industry Trend Analysis**: Regularly engaging with industry news, reports, and forecasts can provide insights into future skill demands and technological advancements.

- **Networking and Professional Engagement**: Conversations with peers, mentors, and industry leaders can offer valuable perspectives on evolving trends and essential skills.

- **Continuous Professional Education**: Participating in workshops, conferences, and seminars related to one's field can expose professionals to new ideas and skills.

Avenues for Professional Development

Once emerging skill requirements are identified, the next step is exploring avenues for professional development. This exploration can take multiple forms, each offering unique benefits:

- **Online Learning Platforms**: Websites like Coursera, edX, and LinkedIn Learning offer courses on a vast array of subjects, providing flexible options for skill acquisition.

- **Formal Education**: For those seeking deeper dives, pursuing further formal education such as certifications, degrees, or specialized training can provide comprehensive knowledge and credentials.

- **Experiential Learning**: Hands-on experiences, whether through new projects, job rotations, or volunteer work, can offer practical skill development opportunities.

- **Peer Learning and Mentorship**: Learning from the experiences and insights of others in your field can complement formal education and self-study.

Integrating Lifelong Learning into Career Strategy

Integrating continuous learning into one's career strategy requires intentionality and a structured approach:

- **Setting Learning Goals**: Aligning learning objectives with career goals and industry trends ensures that educational efforts are focused and relevant.

- **Creating a Learning Plan**: Developing a plan that outlines the skills to be acquired, the methods for learning, and a timeline helps in organizing and prioritizing learning activities.

- **Allocating Time for Learning**: Setting aside regular time for professional development activities is crucial. This may involve balancing work commitments with learning or utilizing downtime effectively.

- **Applying Learning**: Applying new knowledge and skills to real-world projects and challenges not only reinforces learning but also demonstrates value to employers.

The Benefits of Continuous Learning

Beyond staying competitive, the benefits of continuous learning extend to personal growth, increased job satisfaction, and the ability to adapt to career changes with confidence. It fosters a mindset of curiosity and openness, essential qualities in a world where change is the norm. Furthermore, the process of learning itself can be rewarding, offering a sense of achievement and the excitement of discovery.

Embracing continuous learning and skill development is indispensable for anyone looking to navigate the complexities of modern career landscapes. It is a journey that requires curiosity, resilience, and a proactive mindset. By aligning continuous learning with personal and professional aspirations, individuals can not only adapt to but also anticipate and shape the future of their careers. The commitment to lifelong learning is, therefore, not just a strategy for professional advancement but a cornerstone of a fulfilling and adaptable career journey.

Conclusion

In the dynamic tapestry of professional development, each thread represents a step, a decision, or a moment of clarity in the journey toward manifesting one's ideal career. As we draw the curtains on this exploration of aligning one's professional path with personal purpose through manifestation, it's essential to recognize that the journey does not conclude here. Instead, it marks the beginning of an empowered pursuit, a continuous endeavor to bring your envisioned career into reality. This final reflection seeks to encourage you, the reader, to take decisive action and trust in your inherent ability to manifest the career of your dreams.

Embracing the Journey of Manifestation

Manifestation, at its core, is an active process—a dance between intention, action, and belief. The journey towards your ideal career is paved with the insights and strategies explored throughout this book, each designed to equip you with the tools needed to navigate the complexities of the professional world. Yet, the essence of manifestation lies not solely in the knowledge acquired but in the application of this knowledge through deliberate, consistent action.

Taking action is the bridge between the possible and the tangible, turning abstract aspirations into concrete achievements. It involves setting clear, focused intentions, cultivating a positive and resilient mindset, and engaging in consistent, aligned actions that propel you towards your goals. Remember, the manifestation of your ideal career is not a passive occurrence but the result of an active, purposeful pursuit.

Trust in Your Ability to Manifest

Trust is the foundation upon which the edifice of manifestation is built. It requires a steadfast belief in your abilities, the value you bring to your chosen field, and the efficacy of your actions. Trusting in your capacity to manifest your ideal career also means embracing uncertainty with confidence, viewing challenges as opportunities for growth, and seeing setbacks as stepping stones rather than stumbling blocks.

This trust is nurtured through self-reflection, continuous learning, and the cultivation of a growth mindset. It is reinforced by celebrating each milestone achieved, no matter how small, and by learning from every experience, whether it leads to success or provides valuable lessons. As you embark on this journey, remember that trust in oneself, coupled with action and intention, forms the triad that fuels the manifestation process.

Overcoming Obstacles with Resilience and Flexibility

The path to manifesting your ideal career will inevitably present obstacles. These challenges, however, are not indicators of failure but opportunities for learning and growth. Cultivating resilience allows you to navigate through these obstacles with grace, emerging stronger and more focused on your goals. Flexibility, on the other hand, ensures that you remain adaptable, open to adjusting your strategies and embracing new opportunities that align with your evolving aspirations.

Embrace each challenge as a teacher, and each failure as a lesson. Let resilience and flexibility be your companions, reminding you that every obstacle overcome brings you one step closer to your ideal career.

The Power of Networking and Community

No manifestation journey is solitary. The power of networking and building a supportive community cannot be overstated. Engage with mentors, peers, and professionals who share or support your vision. Their wisdom, experiences, and encouragement can provide invaluable insights, open doors to new opportunities, and offer support through the highs and lows of your professional journey.

Remember, the manifestation of your ideal career is not just about individual achievement but about contributing to and growing with a community that shares your values and aspirations.

Continuous Learning as a Lifelong Commitment

The commitment to continuous learning and skill development is essential in keeping pace with the ever-evolving demands of the professional world. It ensures that your career path remains aligned with industry trends and personal growth. View learning not as a task but as an enriching experience, a means to expand your horizons, and a way to enhance your value in your chosen field.

Taking the Leap

As you stand at the threshold of manifesting your ideal career, armed with the knowledge, strategies, and insights gained, remember that the power to bring your vision to life lies within you. The journey ahead will require courage, action, and unwavering belief in your abilities.

Take the leap, trust in your capacity to manifest your aspirations, and embark on this journey with confidence and purpose. Your ideal career is not just a distant dream but a potential reality waiting to be realized through manifestation.

In conclusion, the journey of career manifestation is an ongoing process of growth, learning, and adaptation. It is a path marked by intention, empowered by action, and guided by trust in one's ability to shape the future. As you move forward, carry with you the insights and strategies explored, but most importantly, carry with you the belief in your power to manifest the career of your dreams. The journey is yours to embrace, the opportunities yours to seize. Trust in your journey, trust in the process, and trust in yourself.

Embracing the Dynamic Journey Ahead

As we draw the curtains on a comprehensive exploration of aligning personal purpose with professional aspirations, it's crucial to pause and reflect on the essence of this journey. It is not a static path but a dynamic voyage where personal growth and career development dance in harmony, each influencing and enriching the other. This closing chapter serves to reinforce the concept of this journey as an evolving narrative, a story where the characters of personal purpose and professional aspirations grow, transform, and find deeper meaning together.

The Nature of Our Evolving Journey

At the heart of this voyage is the understanding that our personal purpose and professional aspirations are not fixed entities; they are fluid, subject to change as we encounter new experiences, challenges, and insights. This journey is inherently dynamic, with each step forward offering the opportunity to learn more about ourselves, refine our goals, and align our actions with our deepest values and ambitions.

The beauty of this journey lies in its unpredictability and the endless possibilities it presents. It invites us to remain open to change, to embrace the unknown with curiosity and courage, and to view each twist and turn not as a detour but as an integral part of our path to fulfillment.

Cultivating a Harmonious Growth

Achieving harmony between personal purpose and professional aspirations requires a conscious effort to cultivate growth in both areas simultaneously. It calls for:

- **Self-reflection**: Regularly taking stock of our values, passions, and goals ensures that our career choices resonate with our inner selves.

- **Adaptability**: Remaining flexible allows us to navigate the inevitable changes in the job market and in our personal lives with grace and agility.

- **Continuous learning**: Embracing lifelong learning not only enhances our professional capabilities but also contributes to our personal development, enriching our understanding of the world and our place within it.

The Synergy of Purpose and Aspiration

The true magic occurs when personal purpose and professional aspirations not only coexist but synergize, propelling us towards a career that is not just successful by conventional standards but deeply fulfilling on a personal level. This synergy is the cornerstone of a meaningful career, one that reflects our unique strengths, values, and passions, and contributes to our overall well-being and satisfaction.

Strategies for Sustained Alignment

To maintain this alignment over time, consider the following strategies:

- **Vision setting**: Regularly envisioning your ideal professional life can help maintain focus on your long-term objectives, ensuring that your career trajectory remains aligned with your evolving personal purpose.

- **Goal flexibility**: Setting flexible goals allows you to adapt to change while staying true to your core values and aspirations.

- **Mindful decision-making**: Making career decisions with mindfulness ensures that each choice contributes to your overall vision of a harmonious life and career.

Embracing the Journey Ahead

As we conclude, it's important to recognize that the journey of aligning personal purpose with professional aspirations is perpetual. It does not end with the achievement of a certain milestone or the attainment of a specific role. Instead, it's a continuous process of discovery, learning, and growth. It's about finding joy in the journey itself, in the challenges overcome, the skills acquired, and the insights gained.

This dynamic journey, with its ups and downs, successes and setbacks, is a profound journey of self-actualization. It invites us to live and work authentically, to forge a career that resonates with our deepest selves, and to build a life that feels genuinely our own.

In embracing this journey, remember that the convergence of personal purpose and professional aspirations is not just a destination to be reached but a way of traveling. It's about moving forward with intention, openness, and a deep trust in the process of becoming. So, as you step forward into your future, carry with you the knowledge that your purpose and aspirations, like the best of companions, will grow and evolve together, leading you to horizons new and old, familiar and yet to be discovered. This is not just the conclusion of a book but the commencement of a lifelong adventure.

About the Author

Evelyn Meridian is a pioneering figure in the intersection of career coaching and manifestation, dedicated to guiding individuals towards fulfilling their professional and personal goals. With a rich background that spans various sectors, her approach melds practical career strategies with the transformative principles of manifestation, advocating for a deeply aligned career path as the cornerstone of true satisfaction and growth. Evelyn's journey was inspired by her own search for meaning, leading her to delve into psychology, holistic wellness, and manifestation techniques, which she now seamlessly integrates into her coaching and writing.

As an author and coach, Evelyn possesses a remarkable ability to articulate complex ideas with clarity and warmth, making her a trusted companion for those on their journey to professional fulfillment. Her work, notably in "Career Manifestation: Aligning Your Professional Path with Your Personal Purpose," serves as both an inspiration and a practical guide, offering readers the insights and tools needed to navigate their career paths with intention and confidence. Evelyn's voice stands out for its encouragement and empathy, empowering readers to embrace their potential and manifest the career of their dreams.